The MARRIAGE· GO·ROUND

To Cindy & Jim,
God's blessings as
you grow in marriage,

Tina & Dennis

The MARRIAGE· GO·ROUND

DENNIS&TINA KORTE

BETHANY HOUSE PUBLISHERS
MINNEAPOLIS, MINNESOTA 55438

Manuscript edited by Evelyn Bence.

Published by Bethany House Publishers
A Ministry of Bethany Fellowship, Inc.
6820 Auto Club Road, Minneapolis, Minnesota 55438

Library of Congress Cataloging-in-Publication Data

Korte, Dennis.
    The marriage-go-round / Dennis and Tina Korte.
       p.   cm.

    1. Marriage—United States. 2. Marriage—Religious aspects—Christianity. 3. Interpersonal relations. I. Korte, Tina. II. Title.
HQ734.K683   1991
306.81—dc20   91–2233
ISBN 1–55661–082–3   CIP

DENNIS AND TINA KORTE have been leading marriage enrichment retreats, family retreats, and teaching on Christian relationships for well over ten years. Hundreds of struggling couples have received counsel and encouragement through their ministry. Tina has received her M.A. in Pastoral Counseling and M.S. in Developmental Counseling. Dennis is a supervisory chemist for the Special Testing and Research Laboratory for the U.S. Department of Justice, Drug Enforcement Administration. They make their home in northern Virginia and have two grown children.

Contents

*T*hat there should exist one other person in the world toward whom all openness of exchange should establish itself, from whom there should be no concealment; whose body should be as dear to one, in every part, as one's own, with whom there should be no sense of mine or thine, in property or possession; into whose mind one's thoughts should naturally flow . . . and between whom and oneself there should be a spontaneous rebound of sympathy in all the joys and sorrows and experiences of life; such is perhaps one of the dearest wishes of the soul.

A 19th century English author

"Here We Go Again"

Do any of these comments sound familiar?

"Why are we arguing about the same things all the time?"

"Maybe I married the wrong person."

"Did I make a bad choice? Have I been tricked?"

"I don't like some of the things we say and do to each other."

"I don't even know this person I've become."

"Will it ever change? Am I locked in?"

"We're wearing each other down. There must be a better way."

"Can we ever get off this merry-go-round?"

Do you feel frustrated, bogged down, bored, burned out, worn out, empty, hopeless, helpless, lonely, irritated, angry?

Is there a circular, unhealthy pattern to your arguments, your cold silences, or even to your denial of problems? Maybe you can identify in some ways with the pattern Bill and Sue find themselves stuck in.

Sue's done it again, Bill growled to himself. *She's*

written a check and forgotten to record it. He was balancing the checkbook and paying the bills—two jobs he'd told himself he should never again do on the same day— only to discover he had $50.79 less to work with than he'd previously thought.

Then he picked up the telephone bill: $91.30! Scanning the long-distance charges, he saw a fifty-nine minute call to Sue's mother. *Why can't they write to each other? And why does she have to call on a weekday?*

Irritated, he wrote out the check and stuffed it into the envelope. He heard Sue in the next room, laughing at something on TV. Impatiently he grabbed another envelope with yet another bill. *It never stops. These things seem to reproduce right in front of me.* This bill was the Mastercard statement. He slammed his pen on the table and yelled, "Sue!" *When the checking account funds get low, she doesn't have the sense to stop. She goes straight to the plastic.*

Sue cautiously stuck her head in the door, "What do you want, honey?"

"I want you to quit spending money like there's no tomorrow. We're always broke! I get paid. I pay the bills. And then we're broke again. I don't have a payday. It's just an exchange day! This happens every time. Why do we go round and round every month?"

Bill and Sue, and many others like them, are riding what we call the "marriage-go-round," a circular ride that usually leads to hopelessness and despair. I know. My marriage has been there.

I'm writing in the past tense, but not because my husband, Dennis, is no longer around. No, Dennis and I have been married some thirty years, and we discovered a way to get off the marriage-go-round.

What we've learned comes in three stages:

- learning to live with *hope,* not fantasies;
- learning how to *stop* hurtful situations by healthy intervention; and
- stepping out and taking positive *action* for change.

In this book, we want to help you identify where your marriage got off-base. But head knowledge alone won't turn your relationship around. To get off a marriage-go-round you must apply the brakes and step away from the bad habits repeated in your relational patterns. The unhealthy patterns must then be replaced with different ones, which call for new, learned skills.

Dennis and I have embraced new skills as we've received encouragement from other couples. Our marriage-go-round slowed down drastically when we attended a Marriage Encounter in south Florida. For three years we were actively involved as a sharing couple in that program. Subsequently, we attended a Couple Communication Program that led to our teaching communication techniques. We began to see marriages change, disasters prevented. And we saw the Holy Spirit begin to renew men and women.

Seeing others change—and seeing our own marriage come out of the doldrums—was so intriguing that I returned to school for a master of arts in pastoral counseling and a master of science in developmental psychology. To this day our learning continues as God leads us into more knowledge.

To help eliminate confusion for the reader, this book is written in the first-person voice of Tina. But both Dennis and I worked on "our" project, sharing the writing responsibilities. What we learned, processed, and practiced, we have written together.

We have been privileged to present our insights at retreats in major denominations and independent churches—even in prisons. And now we share with you.

There is a message here for couples who are spinning on any number of marriage-go-rounds. You and your spouse may be crazy about each other—still madly in love—but if you were asked, you could list several annoying habits that drive you to distraction. You want to yell, "Stop!"

Perhaps you have "fallen out of love" long ago, but you hang in there, maybe for the sake of the kids. Yet you're worn down, tired, lonely, and you want to know that you're hanging on for good reason.

Your situation may be so bad you find yourself thinking of moving out and securing a lawyer. If that is true, our advice may open your eyes to the root of your problems, but you may need further crisis-intervention help. (See the Appendix: "Do We Need More Help?")

Wherever you are in your marital relationship, join us as we share the insights we've learned.

Presenting: The Self-Guided Tour

As this material started to take shape, Dennis and I remembered the techniques for learning used by the National Park Service, which has made provision for self-guided tours of their parks. We explorers were given a map and asked to follow the trail, reading the signs written by experts—explaining the landscape, the spectacular view, the natural forms of life, both subtle and obvious.

Walking along the trails, we were educated. We left feeling enriched and viewing our surroundings in a new, more intimate way.

In a similar way, we invite you to take a self-guided tour through these pages. Along the way we will point out places to stop where you may gain more insight into your own relationship. You can check to see where life has gotten away from you, leaving you stuck, unable to move ahead. We trust you will end each chapter seeing the beautiful vistas you've overlooked in your current relationship and some of the mountains of joy yet to come.

When you come to a self-guided tour section, stop and spend some time thinking about the questions. Jot down your reactions and share them with your spouse. If you take the time to do this, we're confident you will finish this book enriched, laying claim to the God-given gifts of joy and love in your marriage.

1

The Ride of Your Life

*E*very Memorial Day my older brother, sister, and I officially began our summer vacation with a trip to the Park Point beach on the western shore of Lake Superior. I especially remember the expedition at the end of my first school year, when they dragged me behind them, running toward the merry-go-round.

Standing in line with my ticket tight in my fist, I was hypnotized by the brightly painted ponies, rising and dipping as the ride went round and round. Strings of lights as colorful as a Christmas tree flashed off and on. The fantasy world was completed by the tinny, whistling music of the calliope.

I quickly spotted the horse I wanted to ride and, as soon as the machine stopped, I raced onto the platform and claimed the pony carved with pink and yellow roses looping around and over the long, curly white mane.

To my mind it wasn't a wooden pony; it was a magnificent steed. I hopped up and clung to its pole—for my very life. When we started to move I was swept up and forward—faster and faster, until I was sure we

17

were galloping. And the brass ring. Oh, how I hoped to grab that brass ring! As this great merry-go-round began its circular course, all I could think about was reaching for that shining goal.

At that moment there was no hint that riding a merry-go-round could be anything but pure joy.

I remember another day—two days actually—twelve and thirteen years later, when my excitement and expectation equalled that of my Memorial Day "horse" ride. I had met Dennis Korte on a blind date. I was making pizza in my girlfriend's kitchen when I turned around and there he stood! He was so handsome, dressed in a red, white, and blue softball uniform! He had big, gentle brown eyes, a warm, inviting smile, and a tall, strong build. After spending several hours with him, I realized he was just perfect for me.

I would have married Dennis that night if he had asked, I was so attracted to him. It took him a little longer to feel the same way. Two years later, sitting in his old green Chevrolet, he asked me to marry him. I jumped at the chance to make my dreams come true. He was everything I had wished for, my prince charming.

The day of my wedding finally came. My dad drove me to the church. As we came to the top of the hill overlooking the church, he pulled over to the curb and turned off the ignition. He sat silently for what seemed like forever, while I fidgeted with my white taffeta dress and wedding veil. From the top of the hill, I could see guests arriving at the church. I even caught a glimpse of the dashing figure of my wonderful husband-to-be striding through the rear door. My dad turned to me and said, "It's not too late. Do you want to change your mind? You can, you know." No way! My eyes, my mind, my heart were set to live out a magical life of ecstasy with the man of my dreams. In just a short while fantasy would become reality!

As a girl of eighteen, I had no idea what my dad was really asking. Now I know that he wanted me to reconsider the reasons for getting married. But I felt ready to leave home, to be independent, to get away from him and Mom. I was sure I wouldn't make the same mistakes they had. I wanted my own family and home. I felt safe with Dennis. He had a good job after graduating from college. I knew I could make Dennis happy. It seemed so simple then. Dennis, too, felt ready. If my dad had asked him that question, he would have said that he was tired of saying goodnight at the front door and driving home alone. It was time to get married. Also, sex was a powerful force, and we both agreed that we needed to do something about it.

So What Did You Expect?

Remember what you thought marriage was going to be? Are those images still frozen in your memory?

Spending all your time together.

Romantic walks by moonlight.

Dreaming and planning for the future.

Certain he was all you ever wanted.

Convinced you knew her well.

Maybe you actually envisioned the scene of a typical day:

A cheerful "Good morning." Sipping freshly brewed cups of coffee, she pours the cream over the strawberries as he butters the whole-wheat toast. Seated in the rays of the morning sun, he gazes into her radiant face as she winks knowingly at him. Then they dress for the day and linger over a tender embrace, the memory sustaining them throughout the day. They regret being apart.

That evening husband and wife rush home to greet each other with open arms. After dinner the two fall into cool sheets, oblivious to the world around them. Curling up together, intertwined, he tells her about his day and she shares her secret fears.

Sound like a fairy-tale marriage, made in heaven? When Dennis and I married we believed in the fantasy marriage. Girl meets boy. They fall in love and marry. They live happily ever after.

Our major life problem was over. We had found each other, fallen in love and married! We had promised to love each other forever—and the promise makes the marriage, doesn't it? The rest would just take care of itself. Or so we thought.

And we had more going for us than Cinderella and the prince, whose backgrounds were drastically different. We had so much in common.

Each of us had been raised in families where our parents worked hard to provide a life that was materially better than they had experienced in their childhood. In our dating we discovered that we enjoyed the same friends, social activities, music, and each other's jokes. And like Cinderella and the prince, there was a strong, passionate physical attraction.

And then there was the matter of children. Once a baby arrived, we would be drawn closer—if being closer was even possible.

I have nothing against fairy tales—as long as they stay in storybooks. But there are no storybook marriages. As for merry-go-rounds, Dennis knows even more about them than I.

SELF-GUIDED TOUR

1. *Think back to the person you were when you married. Why did you marry? List one or more reasons.*
2. *Take a few moments to think about your engagement period and wedding. What fairy tales or myths did you believe in? You might write out your own script of what you thought a typical married-life day would be.*

Dennis's Merry-Go-Round Summer

I can't say that I rode the Park Point merry-go-round often enough to despair of the ride. But when Dennis was sixteen, he ran that merry-go-round all summer—three thousand times, seventy-five times a day. The routine: release the brake; start the ride; collect the tickets; watch the timer; slowly apply the brakes. Stop the ride. I want to get off.

The Marriage-Go-Round

When I grew up I discovered that a marriage was in some ways more like Dennis's merry-go-round than my fairy-tale dreams. The realities of the typical-day variety of married-life problems ground my fantasies to dust. What had happened?

After eight years of marriage, our day progressed something like this: We got up at 6:30. I put on the coffee, got the kids dressing. Dennis and I would have cold cereal together, and the kids would sit down when Dennis left at 7:15 to catch his train. (We lived in Chicago at this time.) The kids would head to school at 8:00 and I would dress and jump into the car to get to work by 9:00. (I taught mentally handicapped children during this period of our marriage.) By 3:00 P.M. I was home again when the kids got there. The next three hours until dinner were filled with endless dirty clothes and floors and dishes. Dennis would arrive at 6:30, and we would eat. Then for two or more hours it was homework and TV. After the kids were in bed, Dennis and I would sit silently watching the TV, the same old programs. We said the same old things, "How was your day? Fine. How was your day?" Then we'd retire by 10:30 P.M., with the same old good-night kiss.

My sister went through divorce a few years before this period in our marriage. She had been very unhappily married, and divorce opened up avenues of adventure to her: college, exciting jobs. Although her divorce shocked me, her new lifestyle was tempting to think about. Now as our marriage settled into a dull routine, I began to feel old before my time. Other places and people outside my home seemed to hold the keys to life.

Are You Spinning in Circles?

The scene in your house on your eighth anniversary will no doubt be different from ours. But sometime in every marriage the rose-colored glasses of fantasy are knocked off and two people are left with a sight that is confusing and frightening, leaving them feeling downright unhappy. Forget the fresh-brewed coffee; just jump in the hot shower—and out the door. Forget the snuggling; a simple, civil "goodnight" will do.

What started with a disagreement about his leaving the toilet seat up compounds. He doesn't want to talk anymore. She's sick of chauffeuring the kids to all their sports events. He's gotten tight with the money. She has a headache every night. He didn't remember their last anniversary. If she has to eat one more of her mother-in-law's meat loafs, she'll gag!

In your heart of hearts you may have known that your expectations were high. But you never expected reality to dip quite so low. The partner you married no longer seems to be the ally you promised to love faithfully at the altar. He or she seems to be the enemy in a relationship in which you are hopelessly bound together. Maybe every day is the "worst yet"—until you actually wonder if the relationship itself is "terminally sick."

"Round and round it goes—and where it stops nobody knows."

SELF-GUIDED TOUR

How different is your marriage from what you expected? Write out a brief paragraph describing a real-life day in your marriage—two, five, or ten years after the wedding clothes came off.

So Now What?

No matter how unchangeable your situation may seem, there is hope. You *can* get off the marriage-go-round. The Bible says marriage can be wonderful: "The two will become one flesh" (Matt. 19:5; Mark 10:8; 1

Cor. 6:16; Gen. 2:24). Repeated four times in Scripture, this God-given promise of intimacy and love is yours to latch on to.

And in the remainder of this book, we want to show you how to move from the status quo to the reality of this promise.

You will see how you got into the circular ruts in the first place; how your expectations and habits fuel the spinning patterns. Even though you may think your spouse is the problem, you have the opportunity—even responsibility—to put the brakes on the marriage-go-round. You can slow things down and then build new, healthy patterns—for communicating, for resolving conflicts, for living together in harmony.

Stay tuned to learn how.

2

First Things First

*B*efore we get to the nitty-gritty, hands-on advice for improving any marriage, we need to look at some basic attitudes of the heart. Where does renewal of a marriage start? With hope.

Right now you may be feeling like a prisoner of marriage, but God, in Zechariah 9:12, calls His people to be "prisoners of hope." The verse continues, "Even now I announce that I will restore twice as much to you." If we were to relate that twofold promise to marriage, we might hope for intimacy and love.

You may not be convinced. "Yeah, well, I've tried to hope before and it didn't work." If you're feeling that kind of despair, it might be because you're asking the wrong questions and looking in the wrong places.

"Why?" Is Not the Right Question

Do these questions sound familiar?

"Why doesn't God change my spouse?"
"Why can't I do what I want?"

"Why am I so unhappy?"

The problem is, we tend to ask only the why questions we answer from our limited point of view. We tell ourselves what we want to hear, and look for solutions based on wishful thinking.

Take the question "Why am I unhappy?" The answer, "Because I go to work all day, then come home and do all the housework while my husband reads the paper and watches TV all evening. If he would change, I would be happy."

But chances are that this woman would be unhappy even if she got her husband to wash all the dirty dishes and laundry. Then she would think her hope was based on her ability to get him to change—which is a dead end leading to despair.

What Is the Right Question?

Hope that doesn't lead to disappointment starts by asking: In what will I put my hope?

Of course there is a right and wrong answer to this question. Let me share the story of one woman whose marriage ended because her hope was in the wrong place.

They looked the perfect pair: a custom-built home, with an Alpha Romeo and a BMW parked in the driveway. Last fall he gave her a blue fox jacket and a mink coat. He's the first vice-president of his company, being groomed for the top post. Though she's my age, she looks like a kid. (She had her eyes done last year and plans to have a tummy tuck next year.)

With the kids in college, the couple had more time

to themselves—a weekend in Vegas, then Mexico, then Florida. They had a summer house in Maine.

Then out of the clear blue she called: Could I pick up the newspapers for a week? She was leaving. "It's over. The fun is over and so is the marriage."

We were shocked. Appearances told us so little about the real situation—an apparently empty relationship. Had financial success robbed them of a marriage of substance? Had they chosen a good time over times of deepening, another vacation over struggling through the "empty nest," another face-lift over dealing with the challenges of aging together?

Because the fun was gone, her *hope* was gone. Her quick, easy approach to life was like a pirate map leading to no treasure.

There are many false things in which we can place our hope. For some, hope comes from material possessions and money. If we're "secure" enough—if we have enough money, enough prestige, if we keep busy enough, our problems will disappear.

Jesus knew how faulty this reasoning was. In Luke 12, He told the parable of the rich fool who had a good harvest, so good that his barns were not big enough to hold it. Thinking himself wise, he built more barns so he'd have plenty stored away for many years. Then he decided he could "take life easy; eat, drink and be merry" (v. 19). In the context of this story Jesus said, "Watch out! Be on your guard against all kinds of greed; a man's life does not consist in the abundance of his possessions" (v. 15).

Are there other false hopes in marriage? A manipulating or controlling person will place hope in *self*. A marriage partner determined to "tough it out" might place hope in his or her wedding vows—to love and cherish.

But when our own solutions fail, when we lose confidence in our own ability to control or to make a change, then comes despair. We lose hope in everything.

A Sure Hope

Proverbs 16:9 summarizes the futility of these false and faltering hopes: "In his heart a man plans his course, but the Lord determines his steps." Here Solomon tells us that trusting in our own plans is false hope. Our trust needs to be squarely placed in "Christ Jesus our hope" (1 Tim. 1:1).

Some of us have to be pushed to extremes before we allow God to take charge in our marriage. But God is *for* your marriage. He's *for* you. He has a blueprint for you to follow, and the plans don't call for life on a merry-go-round. The Bible is full of images of life as an adventure in growth, a process taking us toward an ever-higher goal.

Consider God's promise in Jeremiah 29:11: "I know the plans I have for you, plans to prosper you and not to harm you, plans to give you hope and a future."

That means, where you are today doesn't need to be where you will be a month from now. As Jim and Evelyn Whitehead say in their book *Marrying Well: Stages on the Journey of Christian Marriage*:

> The continuing shifts and challenges of a maturing marriage give it the appearance of a journey. Marriage as a journey suggests that this relationship is not a location in life but a pattern of movement. Marriage is not a place where we live but

a way that we travel through life.[1]

God has set before you an adventure in living and loving, a celebration that outlives the honeymoon. As noted Christian psychologist Paul Tournier says in *The Adventure of Living:* "God wants us all to find fulfillment in our lives, to live this real life and not dream of a different one. And to seek to live it under God is to fulfill our human destiny, a great adventure directed by God."[2]

God is in the redeeming business. Psalm 40:2–3 is just one of many references to the new life He wants to give:

> He lifted me . . .
> out of the mud and mire;
> he set my feet on a rock
> and gave me a firm place to stand.
> He put a new song in my mouth,
> a hymn of praise to our God.

That new song can be one of praise as He begins to renew the relationship you have with your spouse. You don't need a new spouse—or a new house—to live in a realistic hope of a satisfying marital relationship. You need to plant your hope firmly in God. If He has a hope and future for your marriage, isn't it time to be sure you know what His plans are?

---

[1] Jim and Evelyn Whitehead, *Marrying Well: Stages on the Journey of Christian Marriage* (Garden City, N.Y.: Image Books), 1983), 98.
[2] Paul Tournier, *The Adventure of Living* (New York, N.Y.: Harper & Row), 1965, 138.

SELF-GUIDED TOUR

1. *Think again of that line in the traditional marriage ceremony: "forsaking all others . . ." As we see it, the line should be "forsaking all other substitutions for fulfillment—which includes money, things, and busyness that can never satisfy." Are there ways you have filled your life with false hopes— substitutes for the plan God has for your marriage?*

2. *Many Christians are familiar with Hebrews 13:5b: "Never will I leave you; never will I forsake you." But you may not know that the first half of the verse says, "Keep your lives free from the love of money and be content with what you have, because God has said. . . ." God knows that activity, success, and acquisitions will fail us; they will not ultimately fill the void within you or solve your problems. Where have you placed your hopes? in a busy lifestyle, achievements, money, house, car? Have they failed to enrich your relationship with your spouse?*

The God-Given Hope for Intimacy

Because God wants your marriage to grow and succeed, you can dare to hope that you will someday enjoy deeper intimacy with your spouse. You can realistically hope to know and accept your spouse just as he or she is and, in turn, be known just as you are.

Marriage is God's creative design for daily life. In Genesis 2:18, the Lord said: "It is not good for the man to be alone." Even Adam, who walked and talked with God daily, needed intimacy with a flesh-partner like himself.

One of the greatest human adventures is to come to know another who is made in God's image—like us in so many ways, but yet so different. What makes your spouse different from you? There are the physical and emotional differences between the sexes.

The King James Version of the Old Testament uses a verb for sexual intercourse that now seems quaint: "And Adam knew Eve" (Gen. 4:1). "And Cain knew his wife" (Gen. 4:17). "And Adam knew his wife again" (Gen. 4:25). Each "knowing" produced a child, a guarantee that the human race would multiply, replenishing the earth as God had commanded.

To know—as God intends—means to discover marriage as it was intended to be. It involves sexual union that calls forth both physical and *emotional* oneness.

Sex in marriage is fantastic, but sex alone doesn't guarantee intimacy. Andy and Jessica had been married for eighteen months. Sex, from a physical point of view, drew them together constantly, many times a week. But intimacy from an emotional oneness still eluded them. They were miles apart, in two different worlds in almost every other aspect of their relationship, like how to raise their child, how and when they expected to eat, what kind of car to drive, bedtimes and alarm clock times. It took them a while to realize that marriage goes beyond good sex.

What is the intimacy you can hope for? David Mace, a Christian and an internationally known marriage counselor, author and advocate of marriage enrichment, has described intimacy as a *"shared privacy"* that encompasses so much more than sex. We see intimacy as two people being friends, standing side by side. At the same time they are lovers, standing face to face. Though the

31

literal, physical image may be impossible, the relational, soul image is not only possible, it is God's intent for marriage.

Writing of her marriage to Peter Marshall, Catherine Marshall in *A Man Called Peter* identified another element of the intimacy a husband and wife can hope for: *shared destiny.* "Into our marriage came an ever deepening fusion of heart and mind, though never a static peace. It was a harmony growing out of diversity in unity. We came to see this oneness between us as the open door by which the Spirit of God poured into our lives and work."[3]

We have within us the very image of God. What a joy to know that God means for you to discover His image in the one to whom you've committed your life.

The God-Given Hope for Love

At this point, this may sound like unrealistic, wishful thinking, but the love that is God ("God is love," says 1 John 4:8) can be the love you have toward your spouse.

How does God love?

"He first loved us" (1 John 4:19).

It is hard for many people to grasp the depths of God's love for them—or their spouses. Romans 5:7–8 is a clear statement of reality: "Very rarely will anyone die for a righteous man, though for a good man someone might possibly dare to die. But God demonstrates his own love for us in this: While we were still sinners, Christ died for us."

What does that mean? God still loves people who

---

[3]Catherine Marshall, *A Man Called Peter* (New York, N.Y.: McGraw-Hill Book Company Inc., 1951), 227.

fail Him—which includes you and me. "For all have sinned and fall short of the glory of God" (Rom. 3:23). Even when we were not all that God wanted us to be, He responded with love. He took us "as is." (God does not wear rose-colored glasses!) His response to our disarray, our mistakes, sins, and blunders is *love*—love to the extent that He became one of us and took our sins and their curse of death upon himself.

John 3:16 is such a familiar verse that we find it easy to forget its personal meaning. Read the verse twice, first inserting your name, then the name of your spouse: "For God so loved _____ that he gave his one and only Son, that whoever believes in him shall not perish but have eternal life."

I learned about God's love in Sunday school. Sunday morning church has always been a part of my weekly routine. But I had never seriously considered that Jesus died for me, that He could love me that much, until we moved clear across the country to a strange place, Miami. We began the search for a new church amidst my feelings of depression. I was lonely, afraid. I wasn't even sure of my husband's love. I didn't feel I knew him anymore. It was at a church in Miami that I ran into Christians who actually believed and lived as if they knew Jesus Christ. I began to catch a glimpse of a kind of love I had never previously experienced.

He had died for ME! He loved me that much!

Since a husband and wife each have their own spiritual journey, I'll let Dennis tell you his story. "Although God has always been a part of my life, the reality for me was a remote and judgmental God. I would do some good and feel warm inside, but then I would do something bad and feel alone and spiritually cold. A significant change occurred when I was thirty-five years old on a "Marriage Encounter" weekend in Lantana, Florida. Near the end of the weekend, Tina told me she loved me for who I was, not for the person I might become someday. She said she knew God loved me the same way. This tiny spark started a spiritual fire in me and I will never be cold or alone again."

Have you accepted—do you now accept—His gifts to you: His death, blotting your sins from His sight? His Spirit, dwelling in your spirit? Life eternal in His presence? His lordship over your marriage?

A Trustworthy Guide

When God plants the hope of change within us, it's like seeing a mountain in the distance. We know we'll reach it, because God is leading us—one step at a time. We don't know how long it will take; we don't know what obstacles we'll have to overcome to get there, but we know we can make it. And we know the journey, the process of getting there, will be life expanding.

The hope that is ours is grounded in Christ and anchored in Scripture: "This is a trustworthy saying that deserves full acceptance . . . that we have put our hope in the living God, who is the Savior of all men, and especially of those who believe" (1 Tim. 4:9–10).

This book is about *change.* And the first step toward change is to place God in the equation that makes your marriage. With God in a relationship, a marriage becomes greater than the sum of its parts.

Love may make the world go 'round. And "you and me, baby," may make a marriage go 'round. But it takes "God and you and me" to get off that marriage-go-round and onto a highway headed upward. God wants your marriage and ours to move steadily to a better place.

The beautiful thing, however, is that the road is never identical for any two couples. Every marriage has its own personality. Every couple is as unique as a fingerprint and more complex than atomic fusion. You can't, and should not try to, become a photocopy of any couple, even one you admire as "perfect."

Reach Out, It's Yours

God asks that we reach out to the future—to the "more" that He holds for us.

The gift of hope is ours for the taking—as we take our hands off the control.

Are you ready to take the first step off the marriage-go-round? You will not journey alone. Our God works all things for good for those who love Him (see Rom. 8:28).

SELF-GUIDED TOUR

1. *Where is God in your life?*

2. *Take time right now to pray.*
   Use this as your prayer guide.
   "Lord, you're in charge. What can I do to cooperate with your plan for my marriage?"

3. *Think through the vows you made to your spouse on the day you married. This is what I promised Dennis:*
   I, Tina, take you, Dennis, to be my husband.
   To have and to hold, from this day forward.

For better and for worse,
For richer and for poorer,
In sickness and in health,
To love and to cherish,
Till death parts us.
Therefore I promise my faithfulness.

Though we may not have understood what the years ahead might hold, though we may have had a fairy-tale outlook on the future, we made our promises with a sincere heart. Our marriage was born in hope and it has continued in hope, not in our own strength but in God's.

Read these vows again and pray for hope. Look to God for comfort and guidance in the midst of the "worse," the "poorer," or the "sickness" that seems to threaten your relationship.

4. *Anchor your hope in these Scriptures:*

Romans 5:5: "And hope does not disappoint us, because God has poured out his love into our hearts by the Holy Spirit, whom he has given us."

2 Corinthians 5:17: "If anyone is in Christ, he is a new creation; the old has gone, the new has come!"

1 Timothy 4:9–10: "This is a trustworthy saying that deserves full acceptance . . . that we have put our hope in the living God."

1 Peter 1:3: "Praise be to the God and Father of our Lord Jesus Christ! In his great mercy he has given us new birth into a living hope through the resurrection of Jesus Christ from the dead."

Matthew 19:26: "With man this is impossible, but with God all things are possible."

3

How Did We Get Here?

"We're celebrating our fiftieth anniversary this weekend."

All eyes turned to gaze at the elderly couple who made this announcement on the last day of a marriage seminar. Their white hair distinguished them from the rest of us—all younger, most having been married for four to ten years, several working on their second marriages.

It was obvious that this couple—beaming at each other—had a good marriage. As they'd grown in years, God had drawn them together. All weekend these two had enriched our time—by their sense of humor, their tenderness, their strength, their vital commitment. They reinforced the hope for unity we all shared, the hope we'd all felt on our wedding days.

What surprised us most was this couple's reason for coming to a marriage seminar after a half century as husband and wife: "We decided to come and see what there might be to learn after all these years. We did learn something. And we realized that we have *more* to learn."

It's not hard to imagine that their openness to change gave God room to draw them closer to Him and to each other.

Change starts with hope—that the future can be better than the past. But change calls for more than hope. It calls for conscious effort to make changes.

Are you willing to change?

Many times we want to change the "symptoms" of a problem, but we are afraid or unwilling to attack a problem at its root. For example, a couple may want to stop arguing about money. But the root problem may not be money at all. It may be his lack of motivation coupled with her desire for a better or more secure lifestyle. She may need to manipulate him to feel "safe."

Unfortunately, most of us deal with the immediate problem, maybe because we don't even *see* the root issues. So what happens? We repeat the same arguments and behaviors over and over, digging ourselves into a rut. Soon we have a marriage based on bad habits, rather than on a desire for healthy growth.

To free yourself from the unhealthy relational ruts in which your marriage is stuck, it's important to see how you have slid into bad habits, probably without even knowing it.

The Sad Saga of Habits

You may find it very easy to identify some specific annoying habits of your spouse, like drinking and spilling coffee in the car, listening to the advice of a parent or friend while ignoring your suggestions, or attracting the attention of other men or women "just in fun."

These specific physical actions are easy to observe.

But changing the action alone will not solve the problem. Beneath the *action,* we have to see that each of us has an *inner attitude* about how we relate to others and how we want them to relate to us. Until we see and alter these inner habits, the outer ones will never change.

Before we go any further, let's stop and examine the nature of habits—as a first step in loosening their hold over us.

By definition, a habit is a rut we circle around in until we don't even realize we're doing it. There is also an addictive quality to a habit: The more you repeat a behavior, the more automatic it becomes—which is fine if you've established a good habit but destructive if you've cultivated a bad one.

And more than likely one bad relational habit will set off a chain reaction, prompting a seemingly hopeless ride on the marriage-go-round.

Do any of these chain reactions sound familiar?

Stan is fuming at Janet. "Fill up the gas tank! All I ask is that you not leave the gas tank on E after using the car."

And Janet? When Stan tries to talk about it, she clams up and slams doors and pots and pans.

Gina gently reaches over and tries to fiddle with Tom's hair. Tom says, "Leave me alone. I've had a hard day at work." Later, when Gina climbs into bed, Tom reaches for her. She rolls far to her side of the bed, resentful that any romancing—not romancing really, just sex—always has to be on his terms.

Mary complains—again—to John that he's too hard

on the kids. She always brings up the subject after breakfast when he's leaving for the office. "Grounding him for two weeks? A week, maybe, but two? Don't you think . . ."

John scowls and heads out the door, "If you don't like the way I discipline, then do it yourself."

These three couples—and millions like them—have accumulated bad habits that need to be stopped and then replaced with new skills for relating. John Scully said, "We are measured not by how much we learn, but how much we unlearn."[1]

First Things First (and Last)

How do you begin to change—dig out—a relational habit? It is important, first, to know what you're going after. Why does a surgeon spend years in school? Among other things, that doctor must learn how to distinguish normal tissue from abnormal growth.

Though no two couples are the same, there tend to be patterns in the bad relational habits that couples slip into. Because the patterns established early in a marriage typically lead to deeper patterns later on, let's look at some bad habits you might have formed years ago. They're habits that result from the snow-balling effect of your early unrealistic expectations of marriage and your spouse.

The four gospels give a good example of a people's outlook being clouded by their unrealistic expectations. The Jewish people, feeling bound by foreign occupa-

[1]John Scully, *Odyssey* (New York: Harper & Row, 1987).

tion, expected a Messiah who would overthrow the Romans and declare himself national king. The Judeans, who saw themselves as far superior to the Galileans, assumed this king would be one of them. Because they so much wanted a zealot, they missed the Son of God in their midst—not a *macho* man in battle fatigues, but a trained tradesman who took to healing the sick.

Jesus actually was the fulfillment of their deepest longings—He offered them inner freedom beyond their comprehension—but they missed Him because they were expecting the fulfillment of some predetermined, unrealistic image.

Early on in your marriage, for one reason or another, you may have *missed* who your spouse really is. When you walk into marriage with rose-colored glasses firmly planted on your nose, you carry a script, a hidden agenda of who you want your spouse to be. You may hardly know it exists, and your spouse knows less about your agenda than you do. But it's there—to be discovered in time.

Bad Habit:
I Expect You to Do What My Parent Did—or Didn't Do

"When I married Ken, I expected him to be fixing everything," says Mary. "My father spent his time at home, repairing and painting around the house. He loved it. And I have such warm memories of being close to him, laughing and making things together."

Ken pipes in: "I can fix things. I'm probably even good at it. But I hate it."

For Ken and Mary this one issue became a bad scene. She honestly believed that working on the house would bring them together. Isn't that how it had worked with her and Dad? But Ken didn't pal around with her on a fix-it project. Actually, things got pretty tense when they tried it. He felt pressure from her that he really didn't understand. *What's the big deal?* he wondered, while she was blaming Ken for all the tension in the air.

For both of them weekends often ended with a sigh of relief, both eager to go back to work on Monday.

Judy sought out counseling because her expectations for a traditional household—like her parents'—were not being met. "I want to stay at home with our two kids, but Ron wants me to go to work. It's Ron's job to support us. This marriage isn't working and it's his fault."

The family life, the house, the standard of living that she had experienced with her parents had given her a wonderful goal, but an unrealistic perspective on what her and Ron's marriage should be at this time in their lives. Ron was not her father, and her demands were causing unhealthy tension in the relationship.

Your childhood home has a direct impact on your relationship with your spouse. Where did you learn what a home should—or shouldn't—be like? Where did you most regularly see how a husband and wife relate to each other? How conflicts are resolved? Where did you stash away potent memories that are pleasant or embarrassing or painful—circumstances you wish you could repeat or avoid at all costs?

As a teenager Mary Jo was terribly embarrassed by her parents' open affection—holding hands, hugging and kissing, "acting like a couple of newlyweds," she says.

Now married herself, Mary Jo would reluctantly hold her husband's hand for a few minutes and then find some reason to move away. He wanted to show her affection. She didn't want to repeat the "embarrassing" pattern of her parents' behavior.

I had my own expectations of Dennis based on patterns I saw in my parents when I was a child. As I grew up, everyone was expected to be seated for dinner precisely at 6:30. You never had to ask when dinner would be ready. You knew, and you were there. If for some exceptional reason you weren't, they ate without you. There was a sacredness about the dinner hour.

Dennis's family didn't see dinner as a big deal. His dad, a switchman on the railroad, worked different shifts. Sometimes he was there; sometimes he wasn't. Sometimes they watched TV while they ate. Conversation wasn't encouraged.

In our marriage, I grew frustrated over the years. It was always such a hassle to get everyone at the table to eat at the same time. I'd serve dinner, but Dennis wouldn't be ready to eat. And he had no understanding of why it might be so important for me to have everyone there—at the right time. It was important to me because it had been ingrained in me that this was the way it should be. Period.

SELF-GUIDED TOUR

1. *Think in terms of the daily domestic routine of your household. List one or more things you wish your spouse did more like your parents.*

43

2. *Still thinking in terms of the daily domestic routine, list one or more things you think your spouse expects you to do as his or her parent did.*

3. *Think in terms of broader sex-related roles. What expectations of your spouse were based on your parents' roles?*

4. *Think of your child or teen years. Did your parent(s) do things that you told yourself you would never do? How does your reaction to that parental pattern influence your current relationship with your spouse?*

5. *Have you discovered any parental-based expectations that you have not shared with your spouse? Write them down.*

Bad Habit Double-Header:
I Expect You to Be Who I Thought You Were: I Pretend to Be Who You Want Me to Be

Some time after the wedding there is an inevitable letdown for each of us. The specifics differ, but the scenario goes something like this: You're surprised, even disappointed, that this person who always seemed so civilized actually passes gas and picks his or her nose. You thought you were getting a thoroughbred; now you think you really got a mongrel. How does the wonderful prince or princess of the "marriage made in heaven" become the rat or the shrew? You ask, "Did I make a bad choice? Have I been tricked? Did I marry wrong?"

In some ways it's only natural that love is blind. You want to put your best foot forward. You want to impress this person who has caught your eye. You quickly determine what he or she likes to see and you aim to please.

"I wanted to marry a beautiful, sophisticated woman. When Gloria came into my life, she looked stunning. I thought she would always look good just for me!

"Since we married, Gloria says she hasn't got enough time or money to fuss with her hair every day. I wish she'd spend less on books and give me back the girl I married."

"A generous man, that's what I was looking for. Bill was always happy-go-lucky and free with his money, bringing me flowers, buying me jewelry . . .

"After the wedding, happy-go-lucky Bill closed up his wallet. Now he's such a tight wad. I wonder if he really loves me any more."

"What I wanted most was a quiet, peaceful life. The months before the wedding Betty was very shy and willing to agree with anything I wanted to do.

"It didn't take her long to overcome the shyness. She has an opinion about everything. Nag, nag, nag, that's all she does."

Before the wedding these three spouses saw what they wanted to see—a candidate to make all their dreams come true. That in itself is a bad habit. A newlywed may not even realize he or she has unrealistic expectations until a spouse no longer meets them. Then, in time, disillusionment takes its toll.

But there's often a second bad habit that is a Siamese

twin to unrealistic expectations. As much as love is blind, love is dishonest: We often pretend to be what we think someone wants. The three spouses quoted above all discovered a degree of premarital pretense that eventually came off like a mask. Here's what the mates of these people say about those premarital days.

Gloria says, "I knew my Scott was proud of the way I looked. After all, back then I was spending twice as much money and time at the hair dressers."

Bill says, "I work hard and try to save for the future, but when I met Jan I just wanted to take her everywhere and buy her flowers all the time."

Betty smiles, remembering her courtship, "I was so overwhelmed by this big tall guy who had so many plans and ideas. I probably didn't say much of anything the first six months of marriage."

There's a fine line that's easy to step over: Yes, every eligible man or woman wants to be at his or her best in the company of an interesting, interested party of the opposite sex. But how many of us started to pretend to be the person we thought that special someone wanted us to be—only to find ourselves in one of two scenarios? Eventually we were miserable in our dishonesty, or we dropped our mask, to our mate's surprise and disappointment.

The first years of our marriage I thought Dennis expected me to be happy and cheerful—as I had been throughout our courtship and engagement. He had more of a pessimistic temperament. He seemed to need me to be optimistic. If he found out that I didn't always feel like smiling, would he still love me?

But eventually I told him that my smile wasn't always a true reflection of my feelings. He felt tricked, deceived, angry. He says his first response was, "If Tina wasn't this happy, cheerful, smiling person all the time, then who was she? How had I missed who she really was?"

Believe me, I hadn't meant to be dishonest. I had meant to please the man I loved. Here we were, two people in love, trying to please each other, and yet separated, not knowing who we were.

During her courtship with Don, Jeannie was exceptionally good-natured. After all, she was in love, which is good reason to have a smile. In fact, whenever Don appeared, she grinned from ear to ear. Don always seemed to make her beam. But five years into the marriage, Don shared, "I promised myself that Jeannie would always be happy, unlike my mother who always looked sad. But Jeannie doesn't even smile anymore. I think our marriage is over and it's my fault."

But it wasn't his fault. By nature Jeannie was serious, somber almost. She was an introvert. It's not that she wasn't happy; she just didn't show it. She was happy in little ways, fixing dinner, staying home on the weekends or reading a book. She had never learned how to express whether she was happy, sad or angry. Don's unrealistic expectations of Jeannie always smiling made him try everything he knew to make her happy: bringing her flowers, dragging her to Friday night concerts, and planning their vacation in New York City. But the harder he tried, the more Jeannie felt controlled and boxed in—forced to be someone she was not, which only served to fuel her melancholy.

Don could envision marriage only two ways: If it's

not "perfect," it's not working, and if she isn't happy, she doesn't love me. Jeannie did love him; she just couldn't live up to his expectations.

In short, the unrealistic expectations we have of each other blind us to the reality of the person we have agreed to spend the rest of our lives with. Because we don't know this person, we think he or she doesn't love us.

Bad Habit:
I Don't Articulate My Dreams

A habit closely related to these unrealistic expectations is that of not articulating our dreams. We all have ambitions for success—as we define it, even though our definitions may not be obvious even to ourselves.

Peter, for instance, knew exactly what he wanted from life. "I expected to make my first million by the time I was thirty. I knew this would mean three weeks out of the month on the road, but I thought it was worth it. This would place me at the top of my field. I would be set for life, and it would be good for Judy and our children." In a counseling session he told us his dreams. But had he verbalized them—and the price he'd pay for them—to his wife, Judy? No.

She said, "I want Peter to be successful. I like the new car every year, but I married to have a family. And a family should spend their evenings together, playing and enjoying each other's company." Family time was Judy's definition of success. "Just being together would be enough for me."

SELF-GUIDED TOUR

1. *What unrealistic expectations did you have of your bride or groom? Be specific.*

2. *Did you verbalize your expectations? If not, did you make them known in other ways?*

3. *Did you feel your spouse had unrealistic expectations of you, whether they were verbalized or not?*

4. *Do you now see that you were dishonest—even if your intentions were good—in the days of your courtship or early marriage? What did you pretend to be for your spouse?*
   - ☐ *playboy bunny*
   - ☐ *"I can handle anything" macho man*
   - ☐ *gourmet cook*
   - ☐ *Mr. or Mrs. Clean*
   - ☐ *Mr. Goodwrench*
   - ☐ *Mr. Wonderful or Mrs. I Understand*
   - ☐ *Mr. or Mrs. All Smiles*
   - ☐ _____
   - ☐ _____

5. *What dreams have you had for your future that you have not adequately articulated to your spouse?*

4

Tuning Out

Subsequent layers of bad habits can build on these early expectations of the ones we married. It goes something like this: We assume we know them *so* well . . . Why bother to find out what they're really thinking or who they really are? Why not just tune them out—as we tune in our own thoughts and feelings and self-centered agendas?

Let's look at a few of these bad habits.

Bad Habit Double-Header:
I Think That I Know What You're Thinking:
Ignore Who You Really Are

Let's face it. It's risky business—knowing exactly who this person is who shares your bed. The easiest path is to assume you know the other person's thoughts and to ignore who he or she really is. As I've mentioned, I thought Dennis wanted me to be always happy. Had I ever asked him about it? Of course not. I thought that he thought . . .

This kind of thinking can lead to imaginary conversations that make us mad or sad, for no good reason.

This habit of carrying on inner dialogues developed deep roots in our marriage. I was a master at "I bet that he thinks that I think that . . ." If Dennis didn't arrive home from the office on time, for instance, and he hadn't called to warn me, I would boil inside. Boy would I stew, assuming that he expected me to keep dinner hot, ready for him the minute he walked in the door. "Well, if he thinks that I think that I should keep dinner hot, he is wrong." By the time he got home, I was so angry you would have thought we'd had an all-out verbal fight.

Of course you can always win an imaginary argument—or lose, depending on your temperament. And if you can always control the outcome, you may not see a need to make changes in your habit, even though you spend a great deal of time stomping or moping around the house.

Let me give you my version, then Dennis's, of an evening maybe twenty years ago—an evening doomed to disaster because each of us was "thinking the thoughts of the other."

I remember being so excited. The kids were spending the night with friends, and Dennis and I would have an evening to ourselves. Maybe dinner out, maybe a movie. Surely some intimacy. Though I called Dennis to tell him that the kids would be gone, I didn't mention any of these "maybes." After all, I told myself, he was busy . . .

I was really tired out, having spent the morning helping with the vacation church school. But when I realized that the kids were gone, my energy revived: my chance to scrub and wax the kitchen floor without four little feet running in and out.

As I scrubbed I thought more about the evening ahead. We'd been married ten years. I knew Dennis was not keen on spontaneous adventures. *He likes dinner at home,* I thought. *I'll make a pot of chili, something easy. If we go out, I can always turn it off.*

Tired but anticipating an evening out, I hopped in the shower. When Dennis walked in the door, I was in my bathrobe, stirring the chili. Dennis looked hot and tired from his long commute. We had just moved south to Miami and our car didn't have air conditioning. *I shouldn't make him take me out,* I thought. I continued fixing dinner but all the while hoped he would suggest going out.

He didn't, and our conversation dried up slowly. We drifted toward the dinner table and went through our usual routine as if the children had been there with us. As we ate, my sympathy for his tiredness waned. I started to feel irritated. I was tired too! *Why can't he set aside his tiredness to take me out? He's so selfish. We never go out. We always do things his way.* As this thinking progressed, irritation turned into silent anger.

I cleaned up the kitchen, banging pans and slamming doors, then headed for the family room where I worked on a jigsaw puzzle—alone. When I went to bed he was already there. I quietly crept into my side, careful not to get near his touch.

For days I felt a gulf between us. Anger, self-pity, confusion, unhappiness, loneliness—it was a heavy price to pay for such a small incident. How had my anticipation turned on me so fast? And it was all Dennis's fault. Why hadn't he stopped this before it was so out of hand?

So much for my story. Dennis has a different version:

"Tina called to say that the kids were sleeping over. She didn't say much more than that before someone came in and I had to go.

"On my way home I got to thinking about the evening. Just the two of us. It had been so long. Maybe dinner out. Maybe a movie. The ride home in Miami was always a sweaty affair, but that night I didn't mind it.

"I opened the front door and I smelled chili cooking. Tina had on her robe and looked tired as she gave me a little kiss. I didn't say anything, but I was confused. *Why did she bother to call me at work with the news that the kids were gone tonight? Well, she must have decided that she was too tired to do anything different. Pretty selfish on her part,* I thought, feeling disappointed.

"Dinner was pretty quiet, and afterward I could hear her slamming pots around in the kitchen. *What's her problem? I'm the one who should be upset.*"

Here we were: two people wanting the same good thing, but two people who did not get beyond "I think that he/she thinks . . ." Neither of us asked what the other was thinking; neither of us offered our own thoughts.

SELF-GUIDED TOUR

1. *Why is it easier to second-guess your spouse than to find out what's really going on?*

2. *In what areas do you tend to assume you know*

your spouse's thoughts?

*3. In what areas do you sense that your spouse
   assumes to know what you're thinking?*

Bad Habit:
I Don't Listen to You

Bad habits come in groupings, and thinking your
spouse's thoughts goes hand-in-hand with poor listening. A love community of two is devastated when no
one is listening.

Paul Tournier, a Christian physician and psychia-
trist, was right on when he wrote, "Listen to the conversations of our world, between nations as well as those
between couples. They are for the most part dialogues
of the deaf."[1]

Noted philosophy educator Abraham Kaplan has
painted a graphic picture of communication in our so-
ciety. Called "Duologue," it presents two TV sets
turned on and facing each other. Dennis's interpretation
of what he's saying is that even though we may talk a
lot, we never really listen to each other. It's as if two
people are facing each other and talking; each is tuned
in to a different channel. With no regard to what the
other is saying, each is interested in sending out his or
her own program. It takes conscious effort to pause
from our own preoccupation with self and pay attention
to the person we love. The ultimate in ignoring who
your partner is, is to tune out what he or she is saying.

Perhaps you've realized, in your marriage, that you

---

[1]Paul Tournier, *To Understand Each Other* (Atlanta, Ga.: John Knox Press, 1967).

can be perfectly silent and still not be listening to someone. The question is, do you like it that way?

SELF-GUIDED TOUR

1. *Put a check in each box that describes how you "listen."*
   - ☐ *I hear only what supports my biases. Because I have selective hearing, I sometimes wrongly assume that we agree.*
   - ☐ *I don't actually interrupt, but when my spouse is talking I'm often thinking,* Hurry up and get it out, because I have something really important to say—or do.
   - ☐ *I yawn, leave the room, or change the subject to signal that I don't want to hear you.*
   - ☐ *I'm sure I can daydream and listen at the same time. "Mm, hm, yes dear, I hear you. Anything you say. Do what you think is best." (Later I'm surprised at what my spouse did— and said I approved of. Apparently I heard only bits and pieces and even they didn't register.)*
   - ☐ *If my spouse says something early in a "paragraph" that I disagree with or that reminds me of something else, I stop listening and start planning my own response.*
   - ☐ *I'm very conscious of the way others, including my spouse, pronounce words and put together sentences. It's important for me to correct this poor grammar.*
   - ☐ *What someone says is much more important than the tone with which it's said or the speaker's body language.*
   - ☐ *For any number of reasons I interrupt my spouse*

before he or she is finished expressing a thought or feeling.

Bad Habit:
I Blame You for Anything That's Wrong

The night of the "chili affair," Dennis and I thought we knew what the other was thinking. But there was something else going on. We were quick to blame the other for the tension between us.

"It's your fault." That's a line as old as Adam and Eve. When God confronted the couple for having eaten the forbidden fruit, Adam blamed Eve; Eve blamed the serpent. The blame game was on. What was God's view? He held both Adam and Eve responsible for their personal actions.

Don "always" got home late from work. The repeating pattern went something like this: When Pam was starting supper, Don would call to say he'd been held up. He'd state a time when he expected to get home. So Pam would turn off the meal and finish preparing it so it would be ready when he walked in.

But Don would be delayed longer. Pam's response? "A good meal gets ruined and I get upset. Don apologizes and promises it won't happen again. But I'm getting sick of being treated this way. I work hard too. Why does he take me for granted?"

She was so stuck in the blame rut that the thought that she could change her habits, and not put the final touches on a dinner until Don pulled in the driveway, didn't cross Pam's mind. She could not see another way. As far as she was concerned, the entire problem that kept her anger spinning was *his fault*, totally out of her hands.

This bad habit might be reduced to a twist of an old line: "I've seen the enemy and it is you."

Bad Habit:

I Blame You for Being Different From Me

A closely related habit is one spouse's tendency to blame the other for any differences between them. If you've been married more than two weeks, you *know* there are irritating differences between you. It's as sure as your differing fingerprints or voice tones.

Many of these go back to childhood family patterns, but that doesn't account for all idiosyncracies. Two sisters sharing the same bedroom can be as different as night and day, one being a neat-nik and the other being a slob.

Whether they are inherited or programmed, stereotypical differences between the sexes show up at an early age. Males and females are different. It's obvious that we are not the same in size and anatomy, but beyond that the emerging body of evidence suggests that we hear with different aural responses and even puzzle out problems with different cells in our brains. Research is now being done that validates differences between men and women: how we feel, how we hear, and how we experience our world. Men's brains may make them more visual-spatial, and thus superior in math. Women's brains may make them more verbally disposed. Men appear to be more athletic, aggressive, and rough and tumble. Women are caregivers, the "feelers," with better developed interpersonal skills. Russel Baker, a syndicated columnist, happily puts it this way: "The fact is women are warm and men are hairy."

Why does it seem that opposites attract, even those that aren't in any way sex-linked? Do you remember my fascination with the merry-go-round? It was heightened by the tinny whistling music of the calliope. Well, Dennis hated the calliope. The noise of it only made his summer more intolerable. Do any of these "opposites" describe you and your spouse?

- ☐ One is a clock watcher. The other is always late.
- ☐ One looks at the big picture. The other is worried about the details.
- ☐ One is neat. The other, messy.
- ☐ One wants to give everything away or have an annual yard sale. The other is a chronic "saver." ("I may need it someday.")
- ☐ One is a talker. The other is quietly content.
- ☐ One is always turning the lights on. The other is always turning them off.
- ☐ One is intent on getting a daily dose of exercise. The other dislikes walking around the block.
- ☐ One carefully watches his or her diet. The other eats anything in sight.
- ☐ One is fashion conscious. The other dresses as if he or she were color blind.
- ☐ One sleeps with the window open. The other hates drafts.
- ☐ One loves to vacation at the beach. The other loves the mountains.
- ☐ One loves the excitement of urban life. The other prefers a home on the range.

The bad habits associated with two people's differences are rooted in a spouse's tendency to say, "My way is right. Your way is wrong. If you would just do things my way, everything would be all right."

Stan and Virginia had been married one year, and one issue seemed to symbolize their two warring camps. Voices were rising all out of proportion to the situation at hand. "They belong in the cupboard!" Virginia stated in her best I-shall-not-be-moved tone.

Stan also held his ground. "I want the salt and pepper kept on the table so I can season what I want when I'm eating." Each party was staking out a territory and a mindset that demanded a win-lose battle.

SELF-GUIDED TOUR

1. *Reread the checklist of opposites above. Check which ones apply to your marriage. List any other opposites you can see in your relationship.*

2. *Not all differences are as radical as "opposites." What other differences between you and your spouse do you notice on a daily basis? Which of your differences might be sex-linked?*

Bad Habit:
I Try to Change You

In this misguided spirit of "I'm right and you're wrong," we undertake the business of changing our spouses.

Think about it: How many sermons have you heard that you were sure your spouse needed to hear? What was the last book, tract, or article you left in a handy spot—maybe the bathroom—so your spouse would "get the message"?

I can tell you that I tried to change Dennis—always with our best interests at heart. *We could be so much happier if he would just . . .*

Take the way he dressed. Did I ever complain about his favorite gold corduroy pants? They were the most disgusting . . . too baggy, a putrid color, and—believe it or not—no matter how many times they were washed, they smelled. One day I threw them out. At first, Dennis didn't seem to miss them. But two weeks later he really got angry when he found out that I had tossed them out without asking. He said they were "broken in" and were just right for wearing around the house. I was a little surprised, but they were gone now. *No way to get them back,* I thought gleefully. I held my ground and told him how much I disliked those pants. He stared daggers, then shook his head and walked away, grumbling something about having to "break in" another pair. After that I continued to shop for clothes for him that I liked. (This was tricky—finding something I liked that he would agree to wear.) I had to get this man into fashionable shape.

Dennis had his own ideas of good shape—for himself and for me. He's a jogger and very self-disciplined when it comes to exercise and health. For me? Exercise is boring. It's hard work that's not worth the sweat. Over the years Dennis has spent a great deal of effort trying to convince me to go running with him. First he'd try low-key logic, then more urgent arguments.

How did I react? I'd refuse his invitations, then get irritated. Dennis would get defensive—and our private marriage-go-round would be spinning.

What was the problem? Our intentions were so good. I wanted Dennis to look his best. Dennis wanted me to be as healthy as possible. Yet the more one of us pushed and pulled, the more the other resisted reform.

Though each of us was concerned that his or her own side win, neither of us ever won. There always seemed to be an even score. Score one for Tina. She threw out Dennis's favorite pants and got him to wear clothes she liked. Score one for Dennis. He got Tina to run two mornings in a row. But, inside, each of us was stewing at the other. Two unhappy losers.

SELF-GUIDED TOUR

1. *In what ways have you tried to force your spouse to change?*

2. *When was the last time you were sure you were right and your spouse was wrong? Write out the scenario of what happened, from your point of view. If your spouse is agreeable, have him or her describe the scenario, from his or her point of view. What insights can both of you learn from this exercise?*

3. *When was the last time your spouse insisted on being right, making you in the wrong?*

Bad Habit:
I Expect the Worst of You

Once the marriage-go-round gets twirling, an old bad habit—of unrealistic expectations—can rear its head in a new way. We trade in one set of expectations for another. We see only the negative characteristics of our mates and start to expect the worst of them. We lose all sight of the good qualities this person brings to our relationship.

In our disillusionment, the beliefs we build up are just as unreal as those we saw while wearing the rose-colored glasses. With this bad habit we start to think of our mates in simplistic terms: "You always . . ."

Mimi told me just last week that she had begun reminding her husband of their eighth wedding anniversary. I asked when it was, expecting she'd say next week. She said, "It's in six weeks. I have to start now because he *always* forgets." She told me he had never forgotten because for eight years she had reminded him! Every year she had expected him to louse it up.

Someone who is always expecting the worst is not dealing with reality. This is so easy to do with your children. As they travel through their teenage years (where they challenge your values and find their own), it is easy to believe the symptoms of adolescence—laziness and irresponsibility—are the roots of character. Their behavior is interpreted erroneously as who they really are.

Our son had been given the responsibility of mowing the lawn. With the hot Florida sun and thick St. Augustine grass, it was a welcome relief for Dennis to give away this job. However, their timetables for this job differed. Dennis began to expect the worst, saying, "He just doesn't care. . . . He won't get it done unless I stay on his back. . . . I don't need this hassle. . . . I guess I'll have to do it before it becomes a jungle out there!" We never did get lost in head-high grass because our son invariably seemed to get it done at the last minute.

In time the negative expectations take on the edge of self-fulfilling prophecies. Jay Kesler tells the story of being the houseguest in a home of a family with several boys. After dinner the parents pointed out one son and said they just couldn't handle his acting up. He was such a bad child.

Jay in turn pointed out that all during dinner they had been giving this child negative feedback—telling him he was bad. He asked them to try an experiment. Once a day they should look at this boy and clearly, purposefully say, "I love you."

They did and they couldn't believe the change of behavior they saw. You see, they expected him to be bad—and he was.

Another part of this negative outlook is comparing your spouse to someone else—whom you see through your rose-colored glasses. "I wish you were more like . . ." "Why doesn't she cook more like . . ." Again, with such negative feedback, you're not giving your spouse a chance.

SELF-GUIDED TOUR

1. *Have you categorized your spouse in simplistic terms?*
   - ☐ *Mr. Forgetful*
   - ☐ *The slob*
   - ☐ *The lazy, good-for-nothing*
   - ☐ *All thumbs*
   - ☐ *Mr. Perfect or Mrs. Never Wrong*

□ *The hypochondriac*
□ *The boss*
□ *Miss Don't-Want-to-Get-Your-Fingers-Dirty*
□ *The screamer*
□ _____
□ _____

2. *Write down one positive quality about your spouse.*

5

Here I Stand

*P*atterns for dealing with conflict. We all have them.

For some people they're patterns of escape. For some, patterns of angry confrontation. For others, patterns of guerrilla warfare; you never quite know how or when they'll strike.

First let's consider the "escapists." How do some people try to avoid conflict?

Bad Habit:
I Take the Problem to Friends

Georgia didn't talk to her husband, she talked to her friends. Whenever she and her husband had a fight, she picked up the phone. "Do you know what he did and said last night?" She would end a twenty-minute monologue with a request: "Please pray for him. He really needs it."

For a while I thought I was the only person hearing her story, but in time I realized the church was full of

Georgia's "prayer partners," each knowing the details of her sad marital condition.

But Georgia didn't share with *everyone*. She complained only to people who would sympathize with her—take her side against her husband.

What was Georgia looking for? She hoped someone, somewhere could comfort her and ease the pain, fill the void that was hers because she and her husband were not communicating in any positive manner. She desperately searched for some assurance that she was not alone in her situation.

But where did her tack lead her? Even after a dozen people assured her that she was justified in her complaints, Georgia still felt alone. She eventually alienated her friends, who grew uncomfortable listening to complaints that Georgia should have been expressing to her husband and to God, not to them.

She even alienated her husband from the church, as they all knew what a louse he was. And you can bet several of her prayer partners told more than God about Georgia's home life.

Georgia's household became the setting for the local soap opera.

Some couples take their conflicts to their friends in a more subtle manner. Steve and Christine were always the life of the party—or so they thought. In front of their friends they were always laughing and kidding each other about personal idiosyncrasies.

"Steve is so cute—the way he has to squeeze the toothpaste tube so carefully and neatly."

"When Christine gets up in the morning, half asleep, to make my 'delicious' lunch, she throws a slice of bologna in the air, grabs two pieces of stale bread, and slaps the bread together as the bologna comes down."

One night Steve realized everyone was laughing at this sandwich-making routine—everyone but Christine, who was glaring at him. He told us, "On the way home Christine announced that if I felt that way about her sandwiches, I'd better start making my own." It took weeks for him to convince her that he appreciated her efforts.

In the "safety" of friends and under the guise of a "joke," both Christine and Steve had learned to release some of the tension between them. It worked temporarily, but eventually the cork blew because they didn't directly address the irritations as they came up. As they talked with us it became clear that Christine's anger wasn't aggravated so much at Steve's opinion of her sandwiches as it was at the great deal of time he spent with his softball team.

Bad Habit:
I Take the Problem to Mom

Darlene and Frank had been married twelve years when they came to us for counseling. Both were professionals, still dressed in their office attire. "So I went to my mother's after our big fight last Friday night. What's the big deal? Anytime I want to discuss something, Frank is too busy."

Early in their relationship they'd really enjoyed each other's company. They'd laughed at the same things, had fun with the same activities.

But it didn't take either Frank or Darlene long to realize that there was more to being married than having a good time together. As a young wife, Darlene ran home to mother when she didn't understand Frank's reactions.

Frank was nervously stroking his tie. He looked as if he had kept a mental count of the times Darlene had run to her mother's after a disagreement. Though, according to Frank, Darlene's mother was a pleasant enough woman, she interfered with their relationship. She was hardly an objective listener or adviser. From Mother, Darlene heard what she wanted to hear.

In relying so heavily on her mother as a refuge for solace and advice, Darlene was violating the basic foundation of marriage set forth in Genesis 2:24, and repeated again by Jesus in the Gospels: "A man will leave his father and mother and be united to his wife, and they will become one flesh." The more familiar King James Version uses the rhyming verbs *leave* and *cleave*: leaving one's parents to cleave to one's spouse. In this clinging to each other, a husband and wife become one. In becoming one they discover the intimacy that fills the loneliness that prompts us to look elsewhere for love.

Though this verse directly addresses the husband's need to leave his parents, it also applies to women. In Hebrew and other Eastern cultures it went without saying that a bride would leave her parents—to join the husband's family. It was the husband who might need the scriptural reminder.

Today either spouse can easily be the one who frequently resorts to running the escape route that leads back to Mom, that first refuge from a threatening world.

Bad Habit:
I Escape in Activity and the Pursuit of Possessions

Darlene's running home to Mother was not the only problem Frank and Darlene faced. Frank had an escape route of his own, though he didn't see it as such. After all, the two—having come from homes where money was tight—had agreed that they were both willing to work hard so they could have the finer things in life.

But in time Frank was working a sixty-hour week and taking several law classes at the local university. He says, "I just want to get ahead and be successful, but Darlene won't agree with me. And when we fight, she runs home to Mom."

Darlene's view? "Frank used to be so much fun, but life has gotten so serious. He's always working. When he does give me any time, I'm just one more of his projects. I'm the one failure in his portfolio."

Here's the complaint of another wife: "He's never here. He is either working or hunting or fishing or playing ball or practicing for something, and if he is at home he is watching television—football, basketball, wrestling, the list goes on and on.

"I've tried to get his attention. I even suggested counseling, but he said, 'All couples go through this.' "

Here's her husband's view: "I work hard for a living. She doesn't have to work. What else does she want from me? Is it too much to expect my wife to be home and have dinner on the table? I thought we were doing well—a house, two cars, and children. We both have hobbies. I should be able to do something for myself."

Unfortunately, he didn't want to acknowledge that they had a problem. If he kept busy enough, if he provided a living for his family, what more could a marriage ask of him?

SELF-GUIDED TOUR

1. *To whom do you turn when tensions arise between you and your spouse? To whom do you turn with your personal problems, those not directly related to your marital relationship?*

2. *How do you let these people know of your tensions? Are you forthright in your accusations, like Georgia, or more covert, like Steve and Christine?*

3. *Again, a phrase in our wedding ceremony—and most likely yours—was "forsaking all others . . ." This refers to more than sexual fidelity. If you have not forsaken your parents to cleave to your mate, how might you do this?*

4. *If you have not forsaken all other substitutions for fulfillment, including things and busyness, which can never satisfy, how might you start to do this?*

Bad Habit:
When We Do Fight, I Always React the Same Negative Way

It seems inappropriate to even think of the marital relationships in terms of an arena, yet unfortunately, marriage has become increasingly associated with competition and conflict, two activities that would seem to belong to an arena rather than a loving relationship.

Each of us has acquired patterns for how we deal

with our anger, especially as it plays off the established patterns of someone we've lived with for years. The law of reinforcement states that any behavior followed by a reward will increase the frequency of that behavior in the future. We learn how to get our own way—maybe at a very young age with our parents. Maybe with our spouse as we get to know him or her. It worked last time; it'll work again.

If we can intimidate or manipulate someone with loud accusations, with silence, with guilt, with violence or threats of violence, we can get our own way.

"I'm a failure. Nancy tells me that every day," Roger whispers.

"When I'm angry I just dump my feelings, and then I feel better," Bill says matter-of-factly.

"And then he threw me against the wall," Joyce says, trying to control her pain.

These are extreme cases, but they didn't start out that way. The bad habits escalated, the anger increased, until situations were out of control. In these cases the marriage-go-round was fueled by anger and established patterns.

As David Mace says in *Love and Anger in Marriage:* "I believe that close relationships fail so dismally and so often because the quest for love leads to a series of frustrating experiences which produce so much anger that the love is destroyed and the quest is finally abandoned."[1]

Before we discuss this topic further, take time for another self-guided tour.

---

[1]David Mace, *Love and Anger in Marriage* (Grand Rapids: Zondervan Publishing House, 1982), 56.

SELF-GUIDED TOUR

1. *Think about the way you fight with your spouse. Check the items in the following checklist that describe your role in your arguments.*

   The Withdrawer
   - ☐ *I emotionally or physically withdraw when we have a conflict.*
   - ☐ *I retreat quickly by giving in every time. I don't want to make trouble. Someone gets hurt when you confront an issue. Anger is bad and confrontation is destructive.*
   - ☐ *I hide by telling my spouse what he or she wants to hear. Then I quickly sweep the tension under the rug. Peace at any price.*
   - ☐ *I ignore the "little" tensions; otherwise we'd be fighting all the time. I rationalize away or justify the conflicts.*
   - ☐ *I rehearse my arguments over and over, even though I seldom say a thing. I replay our fights in my mind. I win.*

   The Skeptic
   - ☐ *I am suspicious of disagreements. I get tense when it looks as if we will not agree. I don't trust my spouse and myself. What will happen to me in a fight?*
   - ☐ *I think conflict is hopeless, useless. I don't believe we can change the way we handle disagreements.*
   - ☐ *I brood and worry over a problem.*

   The Victim
   - ☐ *My spouse is the problem. If he or she wouldn't start the fight, there wouldn't be one. The issue is my spouse.*

☐ *I am the blameless victim of irrational attacks.*
☐ *My spouse often attacks me, but I don't mind.*
☐ *I have no courage to confront my spouse.*

The Persecutor
☐ *I know I'm angry at my boss or the kids, but sometimes my mate gets in the way and I take it out on him or her.*
☐ *I can use words in such a way that they devastate. I trample on ideas and feelings, hitting below the belt.*
☐ *I seek my own goals at all costs, without concern for others. I win at all costs; losing is a sign of reduced status, weakness, and loss of self-image. No doubt about it, I'm right.*
☐ *I am good on the offensive. I know how to attack, and counterattack. When the fight gets bigger, I talk louder. I use coercion to get my way. I lash out. Thoughts are short circuited. The conflict escalates and the real issue gets obscured.*
☐ *Conflict is a battle of wits. I know I am smarter and quicker than my spouse; therefore I must be right.*
☐ *I simply match my anger with my spouse's. I make no attempt to stop the escalation of conflict, to defuse it.*
☐ *I call my spouse names to his or her face or mutter them under my breath or to someone else.*
☐ *I use sarcasm. "What would you know about being sensitive?"*
☐ *I draw hasty conclusions.*

The Initiator
☐ *I lecture my spouse. I nag my spouse. I continually question my spouse.*

- [ ] I know the buttons to push to get my spouse upset. I use the past against my spouse in a disagreement. I bring up things best left forgotten.
- [ ] I don't keep the promises I made from the last fight.
- [ ] I bicker and pick, pick, pick. Nothing is too small for me to find fault with.

The Secret Agent
- [ ] I'm too busy to fight.
- [ ] I keep a big distance between me and my spouse when we disagree.
- [ ] I just don't tell my spouse everything. I decide what he or she should know about. I maintain an air of secrecy.
- [ ] I disguise or misrepresent my own needs, plans, and goals. I lie to my spouse, so I get my own way.

The Bullhead
- [ ] I am stubborn. I won't budge from my position in an argument. I am close minded.
- [ ] I jump on the defensive. "Are you calling me a liar?" I am reluctant to admit when I'm wrong or don't know something.
- [ ] I am willful, opinionated, and headstrong. I won't change. That is the way I am and always will be.

2. Think about your parents' fighting style. Do you fight as your mother did? As your father did?

3. Think about the way you related to your parents. Were you able to get your own way with them? Do you use the same tactics to get your way with your spouse?

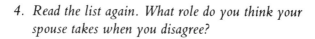

4. Read the list again. What role do you think your spouse takes when you disagree?

5. How is your predictable stance preventing the resolution of the underlying disagreements?

We all have our own way of fighting. We can do it loudly or silently, quickly or eternally, overtly or covertly. Dennis and I are the silent, covert type of fighters. I'm very good at banging pots and slamming doors. Both of us tend to be withdrawers—not wanting to speak the tension we feel.

The fighting patterns can come in any combination. An older couple, married over twenty-five years, had gone around this track for a long time. One was covert and one was overt. She was very quiet, more of the silent fighter. He was very loud and was in command of their arguments. During the argument she would become the victim, and he the persecutor. She held things in but was relentless in her pursuit of what she wanted. He would blow up, have his say, and then become passive in the end. Neither of them ever got what they wanted.

Tony and Marilyn had a different pattern for dealing—or not dealing—with their conflict. When Tony and Marilyn came to see us they'd been married six years, though Marilyn had just moved out. When they'd married, Tony had been a union man, building houses. For several years Marilyn had worked outside the house to support Tony, so he could return to school to better himself in the trade.

Trouble began immediately after they married, as Tony had a hard time accepting Marilyn as the breadwinner. That was his role; he was the boss; he made the decisions. Marilyn saw things differently. She wanted just as much say as Tony in decision making.

Gradually, no matter what Marilyn wanted to do, Tony wanted to do the opposite. What Marilyn usually wanted was change. You might say she was out to change the world, if not the kitchen curtains every few months. Tony, who wanted to call the shots, didn't like change.

Marilyn learned to anticipate Tony's negative responses. When she couldn't win arguments, she bypassed him whenever she could, making her own decisions. She did this by refusing to ask his opinion anymore about household acquisitions. She went out and bought a new washing machine—the one she wanted. She didn't want to go through the negative hassle she always got from him about the price, the make, the size, the color, the delivery, etc. The more Tony sensed he was losing control, the louder and more frequently he said no. Tony and Marilyn had settled into a rut where he was the bullhead and she was the secret agent.

SELF-GUIDED TOUR

1. *Here is a list of the ten things couples say they argue about the most. What do you and your spouse most frequently argue about? Add and subtract from this list to make your own list of the ten areas on which you and your spouse most frequently disagree. How often do you fight about each of these five areas? Do you and your spouse agree that you disagree about these ten things?*

- *finances*
- *household management*
- *personality disagreements*
- *sexual adjustment*
- *sharing household tasks*
- *children*
- *recreation*
- *husband's mother*
- *personal habits*
- *jealousy*

2. *Identify the last two fights you had. What did you fight about and what was the outcome of each?*

3. *Think about the physical environment of your disagreements. Do you always fight in the same place or at the same time of day—over the supper table, when you're riding in the car? What insight does this give you into your conflicts?*

A Word of Warning

None of the patterns for handling conflict previously mentioned in this chapter are healthy, but let me point out several warning signs that indicate your situation may call for outside help.

SELF-GUIDED TOUR

1. *Do you or does your spouse frequently resort to calling the other names, berating his or her character, and/or swearing?*

2. *Do you or does your spouse frequently explode, as if vomiting up angry words?*

79

3. Do you or does your spouse blackmail the other by withholding love, refusing to talk, or withholding sex?

4. Do you or does your spouse ever try to or threaten to punish the other by harming that person's valued possessions?

5. Do your arguments ever include threats of or actual pushing, shoving, or striking? Has either of you ever bruised or physically hurt the other during an argument?

   If your relationship involves any threat of physical violence, your relationship is being stretched too far for you to stop the destructive patterns on your own. Ask your pastor to help you find a qualified counselor.

You were taught, with regard to your former way of life, to put off your old self, which is being corrupted by its deceitful desires; to be made new in the attitude of your minds; and to put on the new self, created to be like God in true righteousness and holiness. (Ephesians 4:22–24)

6

Putting on the Brakes

So you've identified bad habits that have controlled your relationship with your spouse. Identifying them is of little use unless you put a stop to them.

"Oh sure, come stay with us." I was talking with my niece, calling from California and planning a trip East. I didn't think about what I was saying until I put the receiver down. *Oh no, I've done it again. Dennis will really get upset.* For fifteen years I had repeatedly, impulsively invited people to stay at our house. My reasoning seemed so charitable: If someone was coming to town, I couldn't let him or her pay for a motel. Sometimes people would outright ask if they could stay with us. Whatever would they think of me if I said no?

But I'd make the decision and the invitation without consulting Dennis or his schedule. And I did it often enough that it irritated him. He never knew what to expect. It made him feel out of control in his own home—his supposed sanctuary.

Eventually I learned not to tell him about the impending guests until it was absolutely necessary. I figured they might change their minds and not come, so why stir up an unnecessary problem? But predictably, by the time the guests arrived, Dennis and I were not speaking to each other.

When I spontaneously invited our niece that afternoon, I pressed the start button of a very familiar sequence. It started with an invite, and always ended with me handling our company mostly on my own. Dennis would be polite and caring toward the guest but displeased with me. I would end up angry and feeling abandoned. (If this has ever happened to you, isn't it amazing how your spouse can be so warm to the guests in the living room and so cold to you in the bedroom?)

On this particular occasion, for the first time I recognized this bad habit for what it was. And I knew I had to nip it—now. At least I knew that momentarily, while walking into the dining room where Dennis was seated. I had to try to stop my usual way of doing things, but how? *What should I do? What should I say? How far do I have to go? Do I have to stop inviting people altogether?* The thoughts raced.

No. Dennis has to change. This tension is all his fault. If only he loved my niece as I do. No. It's all my niece's fault. If only she hadn't called. She put me in a bad spot. Why does everything have to be so difficult? I don't want to spend the next week feeling isolated from Dennis. The safest thing to do is what I've always done: I won't tell him. Next week before she comes—after all, she could change her mind—I'll casually mention that she might stop by.

Help, Lord. Help. I don't know how to stop this horrible habit.

Let's interrupt this program with Dennis's view of the situation: "I was sitting at the table in the dining room when the phone rang. Tina answered and I could tell it was our niece. It sounded as if she would be visiting us. My reaction was immediately negative. Though our niece was older now, in her teen years our relationship had often been confrontational and angry. I envisioned a tension-filled visit. *Why does she have to come?* I wondered.

"From what I could hear Tina was even encouraging her to come and stay with us. *I can't believe this. Tina knows a visit from her will just stir up problems.*

"Well, actually I could believe it. Tina was doing this all the time, inviting people without asking my opinion. She was so generous that things tended to get out of control."

As I said, this time around our marriage carousel I recognized that I had jump started a bad habit.

Taking Responsibility

You may have recognized your bad habit in an earlier chapter, or you might recognize one later today as you relate to your spouse—right when you enter into an unhealthy situation or while you are in full swing. How can you stop a bad habit—the involuntary action that eventually forces you into isolation, worlds apart from each other?

Let's dispel some wishful thinking you might be having. Couples rarely sit down together and say, "We have a bad habit. Let's slow down and stop this right now." And they almost never stop a bad habit harmoniously and in unison. More than ever at this point your differences will surface, and you must be prepared to make the first move.

You won't stop a bad habit if you base your decision to do so on what your spouse does first. The marriage-go-round is probably not all your fault. It takes two to get things spinning. In our scenario of isolation when guests were invited, I'd start the problem, but Dennis also had a part—blaming and pouting.

If either of us stopped our bad habit, the "go-round" could not continue to spin.

If you try to orchestrate an approach based on "if you'll stop this, I'll stop that," nothing will happen. You'll be waiting for your spouse to make the first move, and you may wait forever. Basing a decision to act on some visible sign of his or her change is really making no decision.

Did Christ wait for us to admit and stop our sin before dying for us? Romans 5:8 gives a clear answer: "But God demonstrates his own love for us in this: While we were still sinners, Christ died for us." For love He took the first hard step, and He asks that we, for love, follow Him in turning from our selfish, sinful ways.

As we counsel couples we often ask, "What part of the responsibility for this bad habit are you willing to accept?" Most often the grudging response from each person is "Okay, I'll accept 10 percent of the blame."

So you have two people accepting 10 percent each. If our calculations are correct, that leaves 80 percent of the blame floating around unclaimed. Because there's more blame than either party will accept, it goes without saying that extra blame is at least subconsciously projected onto the other.

Years ago we heard a story that perfectly illustrates this dilemma: After one of many fights a husband was praying, asking God for help. "Oh, God, please change that woman!"

In the next room the wife was pleading her case, "Oh, Lord, please change that man!"

Hearing the contradictory requests, God became confused and decided not to step into the mess.

Facing My Sin

It's your fault—the accusation is as ancient as the Garden of Eden, when Adam blamed Eve for his own action of eating the forbidden fruit. The history of humanity started with a marriage, harmonious until sin drove a wedge between man and woman, between them and God.

After inviting my niece I had to accept the responsibility for my action. Before this I had always blamed Dennis—totally. If he were just more loving and generous, if he were just a better Christian. But no, my sin was the issue I had to deal with.

What is sin in marriage? Whatever weakens the foundations of the marriage, whatever impairs the daily caring and building of respect in the relationship, whatever obscures the role of God as the central point of the marriage.

What was my sin? Making myself feel good came first, and I tried to please everyone but my family. I was self-centered. Wanting everyone to like me, I couldn't say no to a request. Dennis was only asking me to include him in my plans, to consider the fact that this was his home too.

Ultimately, my sin—all sin—was rooted in selfishness. (Oh, but it was so easy to minimize my bad habit.)

In looking out for me, I had turned my back on the best interests of "we." And my self-centeredness stretched out before me like a road leading to death.

Deuteronomy 30:15, 19–20 calls us away from our self-centeredness: "See, I set before you today life and prosperity, death and destruction. Now choose life, so that you and your children may live and that you may love the Lord your God, listen to his voice, and hold fast to him."

The Bible—the book in which we can find reality—says that "everyone who sins is a slave to sin" (John 8:34). Breaking out of slavery is hard!

Even the apostle Paul felt anguish over his internal struggle: "I do not understand what I do. For what I want to do I do not do, but what I hate I do. . . . For what I do is not the good I want to do; no, the evil I do not want to do—this I keep on doing" (Rom. 7:15, 19). We don't know the specifics of Paul's struggle; it might well have had to do with his relationships with those near to him.

Whatever his sin—bad habit—he knew where to turn for help. "Who will rescue me from this body of death? Thanks be to God—through Jesus Christ our Lord!" (Rom. 7:24–25).

God's help begins with His tender forgiveness. First John 1:9–10, written to Christians—those who have an established familial relationship with God—includes a promise and a warning: "If we confess our sins, he is faithful and just and will forgive us our sins and purify us from all unrighteousness. If we claim we have not sinned, we make him out to be a liar and his word has no place in our lives."

"If we confess" or admit our sins, He will forgive

and purify us. When I cried out to the Lord for help after my niece's phone call, I became aware of my self-ishness, the incessant need to have everyone like me even at my family's expense. I dearly loved Dennis and did not want this to go on any longer. As I slowly walked across the kitchen toward the dining room where he sat, my mind turned again toward God. I knew that if I wanted His help I would have to change my own way of doing this. My way was sin. I stopped in my tracks, hesitating long enough to pray silently to God: *Forgive me for how I've always insisted on my own way in the past. Please help me to find your way this time. And I need your help this very moment as I try to be honest and open with Dennis.*

SELF-GUIDED TOUR

1. *Choose one bad habit you want to stop. Ask the Holy Spirit to help you identify your sin. Write down what you see as your selfishness—your responsibility—for this bad habit.*

2. *In prayer, confess this selfishness before God and tell Him you want to turn from its road leading to marital destruction to a road leading to life.*

Choosing to Forgive

Though I have accepted my responsibility for our go-round when it came to inviting guests, note that I've never said it was 100 percent my responsibility. Dennis did pout and shut me out, showing his displeasure with silence.

For us to make headway in breaking the marriage-go-round, I had to choose to forgive him. In several places in the New Testament, God's forgiveness of us is tied to our forgiveness of others. You find this same connection in the Lord's Prayer. Ephesians 4:32 says: "Be kind and compassionate to one another, forgiving each other, just as in Christ God forgave you." In John 13:34 Jesus said: "Love one another. As I have loved you, so you must love one another."

As you forgive you are freed to renew your love. You might say that forgiveness is the start button of a born-again relationship. Again it is up to you to make the first move—to open the door and let the resentment fly away.

When you choose to forgive, you place God in the midst of the two of you. You choose His compassion over your selfishness. Remember where God's love started? God loved you—sent His Son to die for you—while you were yet a sinner. And we all fall short of what God would have us be (see Rom. 3:23).

Most Christians are familiar with the invitational song traditionally sung at the end of a Billy Graham crusade, "Just As I Am." That's how God accepts us. As is. He knows we will never be perfect.

You—and I—married an incomplete person who needs forgiveness as much as we do. No one, no matter how long a Christian, is all saint. And a touch of God's grace can be seen in the most ungodly person. Saint and sinner—it is what our humanity means. But as we grow in God's love, we become more saintly. And the divine in us calls us to forgive the humanity in others.

Jesus summarizes all the Law in these statements: " 'Love the Lord your God with all your heart and with all your soul and with all your strength and with all your mind'; and, 'Love your neighbor as yourself' " (Luke 10:27). Who is your closest neighbor? The person you married—the one who shares your bed.

Was I ready to forgive Dennis his pouting? I chose to open the door of love to him and open my heart to the Lord: *Father, fill me with your love. Give me the strength to act on your love.*

SELF-GUIDED TOUR

1. *It takes two to spin a marriage-go-round. Choose to put the Lord in the center of your relationship. By doing so you are choosing to love and forgive your spouse for his or her part in your marriage-go-round.*

2. *Take a deep breath, slow down your reactions, and call on Almighty God. Mustering all the help you can find* **stop***.*

   If you spend no time with your spouse, **stop** *doing everything alone.*

   If you have to be right all the time, **stop** *playing God.*

   If you automatically say no, **stop** *the negative response.*

   If you do nothing when you sense something is wrong, **stop** *your inactivity.*

   If you invite guests without your partner's input, **stop***.*

3. *To reenforce your decision:*
   ☐ *Post a note on the refrigerator door.*
   ☐ *Ask your spouse for forgiveness and help.*
   ☐ *Seek godly counsel.*

7

Stepping Out

Stop. Turn. Walk in the opposite direction. It is what repentance—letting go of sinful, bad habits— is all about. The Greek word translated *repentance* is "bigger" than the word for *confession*. Repentance refers to the actions that follow our acknowledgment or confession.

To get off a merry-go-round one has to take the step down off the platform. It's an action that happens at a certain point in time. In a similar vein John R. Mott said, "I never knew a man to overcome a bad habit gradually."

Repent. Turn. That's what John the Baptist preached in the wilderness. It is what Jesus preached; Matthew 4 describes the forty-day temptation that preceded His ministry. Verse 17 says: "From that time on Jesus began to preach, 'Repent, for the kingdom of heaven is near.' "

---
[1]John R. Mott, *Living Quotations* (Minneapolis: Bethany House Publishers, 1982), 102.

Do Not Fear

Again, change can be hard and frightening. Let me encourage you: There is a message in the New Testament that is as basic as repent. It is, "Do not fear." In Matthew 1 it is the angel's word to Joseph in regard to a major change in his life: "Do not be afraid to take Mary home as your wife." In Luke 1 it is the angel's word to Zechariah: "Do not be afraid, your prayer has been heard," and then to Mary, "Do not be afraid, you have found favor with God."

Jesus repeatedly told His followers not to fear but to grasp hold of redemptive risks that lay ahead of them. Actually, in parable form Jesus had strong words for those not willing to invest themselves in a new challenge. Matthew 25 tells the story of three servants and their master, who leaves town and entrusts them with money, each according to his abilities.

Two of the servants invest the money, give the earned proceeds to the master upon his return, and are rewarded with more money and with an invitation to celebrate with their master.

The third servant, out of fear, chooses to bury the money entrusted to him; better to preserve it than to lose it, he explains upon the master's return. But the master sees things differently, calling the man lazy, taking the money away from him, and banishing him.

It's easy to sympathize with this poor man. He was probably just doing what he'd always done—playing it safe, trying to maintain the status quo. As miserable as your situation may be, it may seem preferable to the unknown simply because it is predictable. Anna Sewell once said, "I am never afraid of what I know." How true. It's the unknown that makes us nervous.

Think of the story of the rich young ruler whom Jesus meets (see Luke 18). He seems to want a relationship with God. He asks, "Good teacher, what must I do to inherit eternal life?" (v. 18). But when Jesus tells him what he must give up—the security of his present condition, his riches—the man forfeits the relationship, unwilling to let go. Letting go seems impossible, but note that it's in the context of this story that Jesus says, "What is impossible with men is possible with God" (v. 27).

Choosing to Trust

The afternoon my niece called I knew I had to stop this habit. God had given me a glimpse of honesty about myself. Now I had to make an attempt to be honest with Dennis. This called for making another choice— though it was subconscious at the time. I had to choose to trust God—and Dennis—with the words I would speak. I had to trust Dennis with who I was—as I was.

I knew he loved me. I knew he wanted the best for us.

I did act, though I can't claim that my attempts were characterized by blatant boldness. After my prayer, I furtively walked into the dining room where Dennis was sitting. I stood behind a chair, as if it might protect me like a shield. Time stood still. I remember glancing down at my fingers gripping the back of that chair. I tried to slow down my thoughts.

Dennis was busy writing; I couldn't look directly at him, but I did the best I could to say what I had to say. "Well, er, uh, I think maybe Karen is coming for a visit."

I held my breath. Oh, I had done it.

Dennis looked up at me. For what seemed like forever he didn't say a word—but there was anger in his face.

Though I wanted to run, I didn't. I stayed and faced the unknown. (It truly was the unknown as this wasn't our usual mode of operation!) Dennis immediately sensed that something had happened. He now admits his confusion at this point. "I couldn't see what was going on inside of Tina, and I no longer knew the script," he says. "I didn't know where to go."

Breaking the Secure Patterns

What's the one good thing you can say about a merry-go-round ride? It's predictable and in that sense secure. There's no question about where you might lead that wooden horse. The track is predetermined and you just keep circling. No fear of getting lost or making a wrong turn. No fear of risk.

Breaking bad habits always involves change, and change includes risk. Later on I'll share the resolution of my conflict with Dennis, but now let's look at another marriage-go-round and determine what risks are involved in both spouses breaking their bad habits.

We Fight Even If We Agree

Meet Judy and Larry, a bright, talented couple, dedicated to the Lord. They'd been married several years—the second marriage for both—and had a houseful of children—his, hers, and theirs. From what we could see, here were two happy people with an infectious sense of humor, an evangelistic zeal, and a family centered life-style.

After church one Sunday evening they asked us to meet them for coffee. Maybe we could help them by way of counseling. We noticed that they couldn't agree on what restaurant to go to. That was a clue to the deeper problems that gradually unfolded.

"How can you call me that? You insensitive jerk!" Judy exploded, her face almost as red as her hair. There was fury in her eyes and her hands were shaking at her sides. She jumped up from the table, plowed through the crowded restaurant, and escaped to the dark parking lot.

Larry sat across the table from us, looking ready to blow. His shoulders were back, his nostrils flared, though he quickly regained his professional, lawyer-be-fitting composure. Nervously pulling at his beard he half-jokingly said, "You can see why she needs your help."

Gradually we heard more of the story, from both sides. As Judy began to furnish the house, Larry thought she was spending too much money. He kept his mouth shut as long as he could. Then one night he blew his stack when he came home from work to find a new "pricey lamp" in the living room.

Judy dug in her heels; Larry was being unreasonable; they were off and running. She held her ground. She wanted and needed that lamp. Larry was just as resolute, demanding that she return it.

Larry and Judy didn't fight as Dennis and I tended to—with silent intimidation. They let loose—name calling, shouting, slamming doors. Before the night was over, the lamp was totally forgotten. The issue was simply my side versus your side.

The next morning they were both horrified at the memory of the argument. They both apologized, but they didn't forget the encounter and really wipe the slate clean.

Subsequent "little arguments" seemed to grow out of proportion to the initial disagreements. The attacks became more and more vicious. It was easier and easier to spend more time with the kids, hiding behind them, so they didn't have to face each other. After the fights they would apologize, but eventually the apologies sounded insincere and mechanical, as meaningless as the arguments themselves.

Larry summarized the situation this way: "I was attracted to Judy by her energy and quick wit. But she's used her sharp tongue to attack me, my family, and my kids. There is nothing sacred to her. She has lied to me about her purchases, even hiding them. Now I don't trust her on a very basic level. I want to stay married, but she will have to change."

Judy's version went like this: "Larry is a tough competitor on the job. I respect him for his ability to wheel and deal. When he brought this competition home to our personal lives, I was intimidated at first. Then I figured some things out: If I didn't tell him everything, I could get my own way. Larry always has to have everything his way. He's real pushy. Well, I'm no slouch. To protect myself, I learned to attack first.

"We fight whether I agree with him or not, whether he's right and I'm wrong, or I'm right and he's wrong. So I do what I want because we always fight anyway. The only reason he wants counseling is because he no longer wins all the time. He wants me to change."

SELF-GUIDED TOUR

1. *In this self-guided tour look at Judy and Larry's marriage. What safe and secure bad habits would Judy have to give up to stop the marriage-go-round she's riding? In what way would this be a risk to her?*

2. *What safe and secure bad habits would Larry have to give up to stop the marriage-go-round he's riding? In what way would this be a risk to him?*

3. *Think now of your own marriage, especially in terms of the bad habit you identified and confessed in chapter 6. What risks are involved in your stopping this bad habit? If you have identified several bad habits, identify the risks of two or three of them.*

Looking for Something More

Within a few months of their wedding Jeff and Debra fought all the time but nothing ever got resolved. They both drank, as had their parents, and they could see themselves falling into their parents' bad habits. Believing that the effects of the alcohol caused the arguments, they took a big and bold step. They stopped drinking.

They identified and stopped a bad habit, but it didn't take them long to discover that they needed something more. They were still bickering. Wouldn't it be easier and safer just to go back to their old ways?

At this point they needed two things:

97

1. A vision of the hope for their marriage. Was the intimacy they desired an impossible goal for them? No, it was not.
2. But to enter into that intimacy they needed to establish new patterns of interaction. When you get rid of the bad you must replace it with good.

Jesus spoke of an evil spirit coming out of a man and then returning to the "house" it left. It found the house clean but empty. "Then it goes and takes seven other spirits more wicked than itself, and they go in and live there. And the final condition of that man is worse than the first" (Luke 11:26).

When good habits replace the bad, the bad have no place to which they can return.

Good habits. They sound so desirable, but even they involve risk. "I don't know all there is to know." Such an admission might be easy when the subject area is nuclear physics, an area in which ignorance is acceptable. But when the subject is communication or conflict resolution or loving? Even the suggestion that we might be deficient can raise the call to arms.

Some of us are like the people Jesus described who "loved darkness instead of light" (John 3:19). We don't want to know the better way.

The majority of the bad habits we discussed in chapters 3 through 5 could be eliminated and replaced with new skills in two areas: communications and conflict resolution. If husband and wife are honestly talking and listening to each other, their unrealistic, unspoken expectations start to melt. Reality, not fantasy, becomes a part of daily life.

If husband and wife are honestly talking and listening to each other, "I think that you think that I think . . ." does not become an issue.

If Dennis and I both know why we have different attitudes about mealtimes, we can make attempts to accommodate each other without feeling defensive or blaming the other for gross insensitivity.

If Dennis and I have learned skills for how to resolve our conflicts, we can put each disagreement to bed before we go there, so the sun doesn't go down on our wrath (see Eph. 4:26). We can choose to respond in love, not in self-interest or self-protection.

You can get to know your spouse better. Your spouse can get to know you. You can learn better ways to resolve conflict. The good news is that these skills can be learned. The "bad news," if it can be called such, is that it takes work and calls for stepping out into the no man's land that exists between two people who haven't learned to trust each other.

A Second Look at Trust

How do you take that first step? By putting yourself in the hands of the God you can trust.

> Trust in the Lord with all your heart and lean not on your own understanding; in all your ways acknowledge him, and he will make your paths straight. (Proverbs 3:5–6)

As you trust God, affirm your love for your spouse and your desire to be one with your spouse—to know and be known, as uncomfortable and vulnerable as that may make you feel.

Go ahead and take the plunge.

SELF-GUIDED TOUR

1. *Turn Proverbs 3:5–6 into a prayer, telling God that you want to trust Him as you learn new habits.*

2. *Talk with your spouse, making an initial attempt to open the door to a better relationship. Clearly express your love. Say "I love you." Then take a risk, "I don't know how to share with you, but I want to tell you who I am. Can I trust you?"*

   If your relationship is strained to the limit, the answer you receive may be vague and tentative. But accept any "grace," even if the door is opened just a crack. Remember, your trust is first in your God who can work change in increments so small you can't even see them. Continue to read the rest of this book and trust Him for His help and guidance. Proceed with prayer!

8

The Listening Ear

Welcome to our living room—1970. Our daughter, eight, and our son, six, are off to bed for the night. On a secondhand sofa clothed in homemade, pastel-striped slipcovers, Dennis and I settle in, facing a portable nineteen-inch black and white TV. Finally, some time alone for just the two of us to "celebrate" our marriage.

The typical conversation and accompanying thoughts went something like this.

The TV: In just a moment we'll return to "Mission Impossible," but first a word from our sponsors. (Blast of commercial music.)

Tina: (Eyes glancing at Dennis.) How are you doing? (She slides toward him from the far end of the sofa.)

Dennis: I'm doing okay. How about you? (He stretches his arm along the back of the sofa, inviting her to sit close.)

Tina: I'm doing fine. (She leans closer and gives him

a little kiss on the cheek. Dennis gives her an affectionate squeeze. They look into each other's eyes, paying no attention to the TV commercial.)

The TV: And now back to our show. (Dennis and Tina remain physically close, but their eyes and ears tune in to the TV screen.)

Tina: (Thinking, not speaking, as she watches the screen): We never talk anymore . . . This is a dumb show . . . Why is TV so boring? Night after night we get the kids to bed and stare at the set. I wish we would talk. I had a tough day. Chocolate milk spilled all over everything . . . Aaron breaking that lamp—a wedding present, gone.

My sister, going through her divorce. I feel so scared for her—and for us. (Looking away from the TV, toward Dennis.) I'm so glad I married him. I do love him. He takes good care of me and the kids. I wonder what happened to him today. Does he think of these things too?

Dennis: (Unaware of Tina, other than her physical presence, his attention is focused on the involved plot of this interesting program. Later, he thinks): Tina sure was quiet, and she went right to bed when the news came on. I wonder if she's sick. Maybe she's angry about something. I can't think of anything I've done to upset her. She's probably just tired. Needs a good night's rest. But something's usually bothering her when she gets so quiet.

Two people in love, sitting so close to each other and

102

so far apart. We didn't know how to use the few hours we had each day to get to know each other. A distraction competed for our attention. We now call this time in our relationship our "commercial break romance," because "And now a word from our sponsors" triggered a fleeting exchange of affection but with little talking. A sixty-second intimate moment, repeated a dozen times in an evening. A question, a kiss, and back to the show. My initial "I'm doing fine" could mean any number of things, from "I'm doing great" to "I had a real lousy day."

Twenty years ago, we knew something was missing, but we couldn't identify what it was. We didn't have the time or the skill to discover each other.

It may come as no surprise to you, but physical closeness, even "knowledge" in the Old Testament sense, does not automatically translate into knowledge of another person's heart and mind. I do not know Dennis as a natural result of living with him (and vice versa). We know each other only as we talk and listen to each other.

God has an advantage over us in this regard: "For God sees not as man sees, for man looks at the outward appearance, but the Lord looks at the heart" (1 Sam. 16:7, NASB). But if we mortals are to know each other's heart, we must have both the tools of words and the learned skills of communication.

SELF-GUIDED TOUR

Quickly review the list of bad habits that make up the subtitles in chapters 3, 4, and 5. How many of them ultimately have their roots in you or your spouse not

Is It Any Surprise That Communication Breaks Down?

For a minute let's not assume that one or both parties in a conversation are silent. Let's assume that two people want to communicate. If you break down that communication process, you can see at least seven places where things can go wrong. Each place is like a fork in the road—where the conversation can easily veer off from the intended path.

Let's say you are the initiator of this conversation.

1. The conversation starts in your mind. You think of what you want to say. But somehow, between your head and your mouth, the message took a slight turn. You know that what you meant to say is not exactly what came out. (Maybe if you'd had time to write it down and edit it . . .)

2. Your spouse—the listener—did not physically hear, word for word, exactly what you said. He or she locked on to certain words and phrases and let others slip through the listening sieve.

3. Your spouse places his or her own interpretation on your message. Even if your spouse knows the dictionary definitions of all the words you used, more understanding is needed. Are the two of you thinking of two different definitions of the word—those slight variations that make a dictionary such a long book?

4. Then your spouse must place a personal interpretation on your message: What does it mean to *me*? And what feelings does this surface in me?

5. Your spouse then responds to your message, but

doesn't say exactly what he or she meant to say.

6. You hear the response, but not word for word.

7. You interpret what your spouse said about what you said . . . and the cycle repeats, possibly with more and more emotion and frustration in each round.

Even the simplest communication is subject to an element of confusion. Have you ever driven your car being dependent on someone else to give you directions? "Where do I go from here?" you ask. "Turn, right after the next traffic light," is the response. As you are driving past the light you ask again, "Turn right, here?" "Right" is the response. As you get into the far right-hand lane to make the turn, your passenger asks, in a puzzled tone of voice, "Where are you going?" "I'm turning right here!" "No, we have to go left," your passenger corrects. In exasperation you start to reply, "But you said to turn right . . ."

Stuart Briscoe tells a story of taking his young son to get X-rays. The boy was exceptionally quiet in the car and Stuart asked if there was anything wrong. The terrified, but honest, boy said, "Yes, you can't fool me. I know what an execution is."

Even in the best of circumstances, accurate communication is difficult! It takes energy, focus, and careful clarification. If you've read this far you'll probably agree that your situation is not "the best of circumstances." Accurate communication with your spouse also calls for new skills: new, good habits to replace the old. When Dennis and I were confronted with our bad habits, we had no idea that we could learn skills to enhance what we said and how we said it. For eight years we read books, took classes, attended workshops. We learned how to communicate.

In introducing the bad habits we take on, we said that they, by definition, were not something you did once. Something repeated just three or four times is well on its way to being a habitual, automatic behavior. William James said something done repeatedly for twenty-one days was a habit. Three weeks. In this chapter and the next we'll introduce new skills that must be practiced repeatedly if they are to replace the bad habits you've identified as those that keep your marriage-go-round spinning.

Let's first consider new skills for sending and receiving messages—talking and listening. Though you might think it would be logical to cover talking before listening, I've chosen to reverse the order, for a good reason: A good listener is often the one who is first able to push open the door to good communication. A hammer and crowbar are not the tools needed to get your spouse to talk. And your marriage—your spouse—may not need your advice as much as your listening ear, which provides an atmosphere for love and trust to grow. How can I say "I love you" if I never listen to who you are?

Listen Up!

Statistics show that only 7 percent of an intended message comes across in words. Fifty-five percent of an intended message comes across in body language and facial gestures. Thirty-eight percent comes across in voice inflection.

These statistics have great significance to listeners—on two counts. First, as a listener, I'm "hearing" more by what I see than by what you say. (Remember the childhood game "secret"? Is it any surprise that the sentence whispered right into ears and passed around a circle nearly always became garbled?) Second, my attitude in response to you conveys as much as my verbal response.

What is good listening? It is dying to self, putting aside my agenda and focusing on you. It's becoming a mirror for someone, reflecting back an image of who that person is in your eyes. At its best, listening is anything but a passive activity. It takes time and self-control. In a hard passage about self-control, James said, "Be quick to listen, slow to speak" (James 1:19).

It goes without saying that a good listener listens to him- or herself. This is a perfect place to start practicing Jesus' golden rule: Do unto others as you would have them do unto you. Listen as you would like to be listened unto. Here's how.

Focus your attention on the speaker—for his or her benefit. Let the speaker know you are interested in him or her. Turn off the TV. Don't keep looking at your watch but look the speaker in the eye. Leaning slightly toward a speaker indicates you're with him or her, or reach out and touch your spouse. We've noticed attentive and inattentive couples in restaurants, especially at breakfast. If there's a newspaper present, a sure sign that attention is being paid to the speaker is if the paper has been put aside before the pancakes are served. Other times we've seen the Dagwood and Blondie situation, where the listener doesn't even put the paper down or make eye contact. It's painful to see and certainly isn't funny.

Focus your attention on the speaker—for your benefit. Remember, the spoken words relay only 7 percent of the intended message. What is the speaker's body language telling you? The stance, the stride, the strumming fingers, the smile, frown, laughter, or tears? Dennis has come walking in the door after work for almost thirty years now. I can tell a lot more about him and his day by the *way* he comes in than by the words he says. He almost always says, "Hi, Tina. How's your day been?" He is concerned for me, but if his shoulders are slumped and he walks tiredly, I know without words that it has been a tough day. I'll tell him what's happened to me and then patiently wait until he is ready to share. If his step is crisp and his head high, he still asks about my day first but I can sense his eagerness to share with me some of his excitement. Those times I give him a chance to go first. It's a wonderful day when we both can hardly wait to share!

There's nothing wrong with reading between the lines as long as you clarify what you're reading. (We'll get to that in a minute.)

Keep your mind on the subject at hand. Force yourself to block out other thoughts, even if they seem justified (building up your case of how you're going to respond). If the idea popping into your head is important, you will remember it later. Dennis has told me that he has a problem with constantly turning over in his mind situations from his work place. At those times he has learned to discipline himself to concentrate on our conversation. When we were first married he would try to divide his thoughts, but it was frustratingly clear to me that he was preoccupied. His eyes would sort of glaze over. Now, he tells me if he's got something else on his mind, but that he wants to focus on our conversation and truly listen to me.

Ask questions to get more information. Whether or not the words and the body language "add up" to a message you think you understand, ask questions that help you clarify the speaker's intent. "Do you mean x?" "Are you saying y?" *What* and *how* questions are especially helpful, but stay away from *whys*. Whys can make your spouse defensive, having to find reasons for everything, which is a dangerous way to head when you are looking to be open and honest. Too many whys will shut the door to deeper conversation.

Asking questions that indicate concern can also encourage a nontalker to talk. Again, stay away from the whys. How would you respond to these two scenarios? (1) "Honey, what's happened? You look so tired." (2) "Why do you just lie around the house all the time?"

Remember, the purpose of the questioning is for clarification and to show concern. You are not a prosecuting attorney (or a parent) cross-examining your spouse to try to trip him or her up: What did you do? What did you say? Who was with you? And then what did he say? . . .

For clarification, repeat back what you've heard. You are checking for accuracy and understanding, asking "How well did I hear?" At the same time you are affirming the speaker. Don't add to the message, give advice or criticism. Don't be afraid to be specific and straightforward in your approach: "I heard you say that . . . Am I right?"

Say something that indicates your sensitivity to the speaker's feelings. "What are your feelings about that?" When you receive this information, try to put yourself in his or her shoes. How would you feel? If you would feel differently, this isn't the time for value judgments.

Choose affirming responses. If the message presents an idea that is better than yours, compliment or thank the speaker. If the speaker is your spouse, remember, you are one flesh. You're two people playing on the same team. You don't need to be competing against each other.

You Might Be Surprised

"Out there" it's a cruel enough world. As for here at home, this is the person you've chosen to spend your life with—to strengthen and be strengthened by. Listen and see what surprises you find.

Some will be wonderful and exciting. Some will be unsettling. But as you turn to the Lord for discernment, for His forgiveness and grace, even those "I don't want to hear this" revelations can be used to bring you and your spouse closer to the oneness you desire. To be surprised is to be vulnerable and open to information that may require some change on your part. You may learn something new about your spouse, even something you find uncomfortable. It is acceptable to say, "I need some time to think about what you've just said— it caught me by surprise."

Your spouse may not be the person you've always imagined him or her to be. Those unrealistic expectations may have put him or her in a small box that seemed suffocating. Now is the time to reach out to new and wider vistas, knowing and being known.

If your spouse gives any indication that he or she wants to talk, give your full attention. Turn off the TV or radio. Put down the newspaper or your watering can. Turn off the gas under the frying pan. Supper can wait. Your spouse's courage or desire to speak might not.

SELF-GUIDED TOUR

1. *When was the last time you listened to your spouse with "all your heart"?*

2. *Think of the last time you had a misunderstanding. Would your being a good listener have helped? In what way?*

3. *What time of day and under what circumstances is it easiest for you to be a good listener? In the morning? Evening? In the kitchen with a cup of coffee in your hand? In the bedroom? When you're out walking? How about your spouse?*

4. *Ask your spouse to answer question 1 for you. Consciously determine a time and situation when you will regularly make the effort to give each other listening time.*

5. *Consider your answers to the self-guided tour on page 56. Compare your self-analysis there with the new skills described above. Pinpoint exactly which new listening skills you need to learn and practice to replace the old bad habits.*

6. *Start to be a good listener—today and with your spouse. You might be very straightforward about it, saying, "I want to be a good listener today. Would you tell me about your day and let me practice on you?"*

9

Getting to Know You

*L*earning new listening and responding skills is not the whole recipe for good communication. Our own "commercial break romance" of twenty years ago had two underlying problems. (1) No one was listening. (2) But then no one was talking.

How can I say "I love you" if I never listen to who you are? How can I know who you are if you're not talking?

Some of us, quiet by nature, will always find it easier to listen than speak. To be a good communicator one doesn't have to become a chatterbox. On the other hand, a quiet nature isn't an acceptable excuse, an escape device, for noncommunication. Even if you don't have much to say, you can learn to let your spouse know that you're willing to take the time and make the effort to enhance your two-way communication.

Remember that 7 percent of your message that comes across in words? Well, we believe it's possible—and profitable—to increase that percentage. To minimize misunderstandings, you and your spouse need to

113

learn to verbalize, as clearly as possible, what is going on inside of you. You can learn to make words work for you, not against you.

Let's take a closer look at our patterns of conversation. I like the way David Mace breaks communication into five levels revolving around *what* you want to say and *when* and to *whom* you are saying it. His analysis helps us see how we get to know someone better. In reverse order, ranging 5 to 1, each of his successive levels describes a type of conversation we might have with a progressively exclusive grouping of people.

Social Conversation

The fifth level of communication is the most universal and casual. It is polite small-talk that may not even require a response. Your only intention is to be pleasant. With stranger or friend you say, "Please pass the salt." "Hello, how are you?" "Have you heard the latest joke?"

Using the fourth level of communication, we report the facts, maybe describing what we've seen or heard. (In reality, not everyone cares about what you've seen or experienced.) Your "report" may or may not lead to a longer conversation: "The washer is broken." "It's snowing." "I saw such-and-such movie last night."

At the third level of communication, you share your interpretation of what you've seen, heard, or experienced. The arena widens from facts to opinions, which are an important part of who you are. Because sharing opinions can open the door to people disagreeing with or judging us and because it can lead to lengthy discussions we don't have time for, we are a little more selective in the audience for our opinions. "I bet that store sold me a lemon of a washer." "It's been snowing all week; it will probably snow right through the weekend." "I thought the movie was awful!"

Most of our communication in a day—with co-workers and acquaintances, even family—remains in these first three levels and occurs quite automatically, without much effort, thought, or risk. Before we look at the last two levels, let's stop for a self-guided tour, evaluating your casual conversational style, especially as it relates to your spouse.

SELF-GUIDED TOUR

1. *Check the box next to the statements or paragraphs that describe you.*
   ☐ *I demand to talk now. It doesn't matter where we are or what my spouse is doing. I have something important to say and he or she needs to listen to me. I make these demands known up front, so my spouse knows where I stand.*
   ☐ *I can manipulate most conversations, shifting to another topic before my spouse knows what has happened.*
   ☐ *I overload my spouse with information. I take pride in having lots of knowledge about the issues.*
   ☐ *I really don't have much information about an issue, but I stretch the little knowledge I have. I guess I tell a lot of "fish stories."*
   ☐ *I'm a rambler. I can go on and on about most anything—or nothing. I often put my foot in my mouth. I can't seem to turn off the flow. Kids these days have a word for peers who babble on and on with no apparent point. They*

call such a person a bus driver.

☐ *I always have to have the last word. I decide when a conversation is over.*

2. *Think about the bad habits you checked. How would these make it difficult for your spouse to talk with or listen to you?*

3. *Which of these bad habits describes your spouse's style? Is it easier to see his or her bad habits than your own?*

4. *How do his or her bad habits make it difficult for you to talk with or listen to your spouse?*

Intimate Conversation

There are two more, deeper levels of communication. In levels two and one, our "audience" is drastically reduced.

Level two involves sharing of feelings and emotions. "I am so frustrated with this washer company because I had saved for six months to get that model." "I enjoy it when it snows. I feel peaceful and safe." "I felt angry at that father character in the movie. He was so cruel; I wanted to punch him out!"

Sharing feelings, especially on issues that are close to the heart, is risky business in the minds of many. A recent Roper survey of 3,000 women asked what they would most like to change about men. The number-one response—indicated by 27 percent—was a wish that men were more able to express their feelings. It's hard for many people to find the words to express what they're feeling, even though those feelings usually escape in nonverbal expression, which makes room for massive misunderstanding. ("I think that he thinks that I think . . .")

The first level of communication defines in a way the *intimacy* desired in marriage. It includes the other four levels but goes beyond them to sharing the roots of the feelings—the dreams of the future and memories of the past, the reasons for feelings of success and shame, fear and joy.

"I feel like such a loser. I thought I was buying this washer in such a responsible manner. I shopped for the best price. I read the consumer guides. Now I have to try to get them to take it back. They will argue. I hate to argue. I feel so stupid and manipulated. I wish this would disappear. This always happens to me."

"When it snows it's as if God were putting a pure and fresh blanket over the world. When I was little I loved to sit at the window and watch it come down. I still do. If it snows hard enough, everything else seems to stop. For a moment I feel tucked under a blanket, secure, peaceful, and joyful."

"That movie forced me to remember my father and his terrible temper. I felt angry, then afraid, and finally hopeless because he was never punished. I don't ever want to see a movie like that again."

Think again of marriage as a symbol of Jesus' relationship with His bride, the church. The Bible, especially the Psalms, is full of people freely expressing their feelings to God:

Hear my prayer, O Lord; let my cry for help come to you. Do not hide your face from me when I am in distress. (Psalm 102:1–2)

117

Again in Psalms we have feelings expressed, this time in joy:

O come, let us sing for joy to the Lord: Let us shout joyfully to the rock of our salvation. Let us come before His presence with thanksgiving; let us shout joyfully to Him with psalms. (Psalm 95:1–2, NASB)

These are not examples of level four or five communication to an impersonal, "deaf" God. These are heartfelt feelings expressed to one with whom the psalmist had a deep and trusting relationship.

And Jesus—God in flesh—freely expressed His emotions—joy (Luke 10:21), sorrow and tears (Luke 19:41). In Gethsemane He told His closest friends, "My soul is overwhelmed with sorrow to the point of death" (Mark 14:34).

Though you may feel that God is silent when it comes to level-one communication, let me again quote Paul, describing a future day—after the wedding day of Christ and the church takes place: "Now we see but a poor reflection as in a mirror; then we shall see face to face. Now I know in part; then I shall know fully, even as I am fully known" (1 Cor. 13:12). I don't mind expressing my feeling: Anticipating that future intimacy overwhelms me with joy.

The Mystery of Emotion

There is a mystery to emotions. First, they are subject to every wind that blows. The mercurial nature of feelings is part of what makes them so frightening—and/or exciting—to ourselves and those around us. I can be angry one hour and laughing the next. One feeling isn't right and the other wrong. Feelings in themselves are never right or wrong. They just are. (How I express or act out those feelings may be right or wrong.)

Second, my feelings will never be exactly the same as another person's, no matter how well we know each other. An airplane ride could fill me with terror. The same ride could exhilarate Dennis, eager for adventure. Your feelings are internal—within you; they are not part of the objective situation you are in.

The airplane doesn't cause my fear. When I am angry with Dennis, he doesn't cause my anger. Something or someone may trigger an emotion in me, but it's my past experience, my acquired knowledge, maybe my natural instincts that cause the emotion. I anticipate that ice cream will make me happy today because it made me happy yesterday.

The third mystery of emotion is this: Even if two people say they were feeling the same emotion, let's say happiness, they are likely to have two different ways of expressing it. I might giggle. You might sing. A third person might go on a shopping spree.

Feelings and Wants

If your feelings are mercurial, think about how they are often intertwined with your wants. Yesterday I may have wanted Dennis to be especially sensitive and tender. But today I have changed. I may want to succeed in some difficult task and am fearful or hesitant. Now I want him to be a forceful encourager. How will he know unless I tell him how I'm feeling and what I want for today?

Knowing—and Sharing—My Feelings and Wants

If I'm going to share my feelings or wants with you, I need to know what I'm feeling and wanting. This may take more analysis than some of us are used to. Sometimes we can identify how we're feeling emotionally by evaluating how we're feeling physically. This is where I began in my search for feelings. If I felt physically tired, I would look for words that would describe that tiredness, like exhausted, weary, or run down. Often this would lead to other feelings like too much to do, not enough time, hurried, alone, or hopeless. Our bodies are often a clue to some hidden emotions we find hard to express.

To share emotions effectively, I need to put vague generalities into words. At one point we relied on a list of "feeling" words—adjectives—that described a broad range of emotions. If we could not quickly identify what we were feeling, the list gave us a jumping-off place. It narrowed the universe of words down to a manageable size. On pages 122–123 you will find a list of feeling words that you might use for reference.

A more complicated method for identifying—and sharing—feelings is to think in terms of analogies or metaphors.

- "I feel silly like a child splashing through mud puddles."
- "I'm getting tired, like a rundown battery."
- "My anger is like a storm about to lash out of menacing dark clouds."
- "I feel as joyful as an expectant five year old on Christmas morning."

I say this method is more complicated for two reasons. You might have a hard time thinking of the analogy. Also, your pleasant or unpleasant association might be opposite from your listener's. Remember Dennis's and my reactions to the Park Point merry-go-round? An analogy might call for further elaboration, but it's a great way to dig at the underlying roots of emotion.

You may need to make a conscious effort to dig up and express those roots of emotion. "When I saw you walk in, I felt silly, because I saw your new cowboy boots and they reminded me of my childhood, when . . ."

To avoid misunderstanding and conflict, own your feelings and speak for yourself. Who's doing the talking? You are. Whose feelings and life situation are you talking about? Yours. Who is responsible for your thoughts, wants, and feelings? You are. So what? So speak out using the word *I*. I was the product of never speaking for myself. I would use broad generalities to express myself, like "Anybody would be offended with what you said." In doing this it was as if I represented the whole world. (I thought it gave me more clout.) It was a hard lesson to learn to say, "I was offended by what you just said." But in doing this, I let the person know that I was the one who was upset. I identified who I was and what was going on inside of me, not the whole world.

Time Out

It takes so little effort to be strangers. On several counts, good, intimate communication calls for time and effort.

POSITIVE FEELINGS			
INTENSE	STRONG	MODERATE	MILD
loved	enchanted	liked	friendly
adored	ardor	cared-for	regarded
idolized	infatuated	esteemed	benevolent
	tender	affectionate	
		found	
alive	vibrant	excited	wide-awake
	independent	patient	at-ease
	capable	strong	relaxed
	happy	gay	comfortable
	great	good	content
	proud	inspired	keen
	gratified	anticipating	amazed
		strong	alert
		amused	sensitive
wanted	worthy	secure	sure
lustful	passionate	yearning	attractive
worthy	admired	popular	approved
pity	sympathetic	peaceful	untroubled
respected	important	appealing	graceful
empathy	concerned	determined	
awed	appreciated		
	consoled		
elation	delighted	pleased	turn-on
enthusiastic	eager	excited	warm
zealous	optimistic	interested	amused
	joyful	jolly	
	courage	relieved	
	hopeful	glad	
courageous	valiant	adventurous	daring
	brave	peaceful	comfortable
	brilliant	intelligent	smart

NEGATIVE FEELINGS

MILD	MODERATE	STRONG	INTENSE
unpopular	suspicious	disgusted	hate
	envious	resentful	unloved
	enmity	bitter	abhor
	aversion	detested	loathed
		fed-up	despised
	dejected		
listless		frustrated	angry
moody	unhappy	sad	hurt
lethargic	bored	depressed	miserable
gloomy	bad	sick	pain
dismal	forlorn	disconsolate	lonely
discontent	disappointed	dissatisfy	cynical
tired	wearied	fatigued	exhausted
indifferent	torn-up	worn-out	worthless
unsure	inadequate	useless	impotent
impatient	ineffectual	weak	futile
dependent	helpless	hopeless	
unimportant	resigned	forlorn	abandoned
	apathetic	rejected	estranged
regretful	shamed	guilty	degraded
bashful	shy	embarrassed	humiliated
self-conscious		inhibited	alienated
	uncomfortable		
puzzled	baffled	bewildered	shocked
edgy	confused	frightened	panicky
upset	nervous	anxious	trapped
reluctant	tempted	dismayed	horrified
timid	tense	apprehensive	afraid
mixed-up	worried	dreadful	scared
	perplexed	apprehensive	terrified
	troubled	disturbed	threatened
sullen	disdainful	antagonistic	furious
provoked	contemptuous	vengeful	furious
	alarmed		
	annoyed	indignant	
	provoked	mad	

First, it takes time to think. In your speech, slow down. You can think much faster than you can speak and, especially if you're feeling great emotion, your heart and mind can get away from you. Remember the admonition of James 1:19: "Be slow to speak." Sometimes thinking through what you want to say before you say it helps you get to the point.

These phrases might help you: "This is the way I see it." "This is my opinion: . . ." "I think this is what is going on: . . ." Express your idea, clarify with your spouse that he or she understood, then move on to the next point.

Second, emotions take time to work through. From experience, we know it's best not to start an emotional conversation that you *know* you will not have time to finish. This is where Dennis and I began our journey to better communication, taking time to express feelings. We started by telling our children that we needed half an hour of "Mom and Dad" time. We took that time in the evening to share feelings. We sat in our living room and struggled to find the words to express who we were by sharing how we had been feeling that day. Eventually, when our children were old enough, we stole out on Saturday mornings for breakfast and our feelings discussion. Sometimes just a "small" change of scenery can promote discussion: Go for a walk, or move from the kitchen to the bedroom.

At one point we had a TV in our bedroom. No more. The TV is never a third party in our conversations. We moved the TV from the bedroom when we discovered that it was a distraction to the evening hours we set aside specifically for sharing. A daily sharing time is ideal. We didn't always have the time. We did manage at least three times a week, a half hour at a stretch. This is the time to teach your children how important their parents' relationship is. They need to form new habits too. Now, the two of you pick a neutral topic, your day, something in the paper, some future event (a holiday or a visit), take the feeling list of words from pages 122–123 and share. It will feel awkward at first, even embarrassing, but GO FOR IT!

Even if the conversation is of relatively minor importance, and even if you have the most attentive and good-listener spouse, you'll be bucking the tide if you interrupt his or her favorite TV program of the week because you want to talk—and it has to be now. Timing for personal sharing is so important. Dennis is a night person, and I'm a morning person. When I try to share who I am first thing in the morning, he is blank. I mean blank! I used to be offended, but no more. I wait until he has truly awakened . . . three o'clock in the afternoon! I have to share quickly, however, because I call it a day by nine o'clock in the evening!

If you want to share intimate conversations you have to control your environment. Shut off the TV, the radio, and noisy appliances, ignore the telephone if it rings, or plan to talk after the kids are in bed. (That never worked for me. I was too pooped to share anything.) All of this creates a special place in time for the two of you. You begin by saying what it is that you want to have happen. "I want to spend just ten minutes [or fifteen, twenty, or thirty] sharing with you tonight."

In the self-guided tour on page 111, did you establish when and where your spouse is the best listener? Use that information to your corporate advantage.

Practical Tips

Larry Christenson says the number-one warning light of dangerous waters in a marriage is silence. This could be based on distrust, fear, apathy, or preoccupation.

Sometimes silence isn't the problem; it's that you're always saying the wrong thing in the wrong way at the wrong time. Throughout our years of formal schooling we get class after class on sentence structure and grammar and punctuation. You might even have taken classes in persuasive or public speaking, but not many people formally learn good conversational patterns. Whatever skills we have, we pick up from observing and hearing others, often our parents. The odds are against us having positive role models in this regard.

Begin to notice how people talk to each other and their body language. How do they initiate a conversation? Some people clear their throat, touch the other person, start talking no matter where they are (even from another room or floor of the house), assume someone will listen to them regardless what is going on around them, stand directly in front of you or shout "Hey you!"

Then again, how do conversations end? It is extremely important that you respect another person's privacy of thought. Don't take for granted that he wants to listen when you want to talk. Give him the courtesy of providing a signal that you are beginning, and that you have finished when you are done. To engage your partner in personal sharing is an invitation to get to know each other better. It is important that your gestures reflect caring and warmth. Look at the person. Be near, use a touch or a squeeze from time to time. Sit close, and when you are finished with what you have to say, verbally say, "I'm done." They will appreciate it. Some people simply stop talking and stand there. Sometimes they give a physical signal, like allowing their hands to drop, resuming reading, or just walking away.

SELF-GUIDED TOUR

1. *If expressing feelings is particularly hard for you or your spouse, consciously spend time communicating at levels three and four—about facts and opinions. You might do this by reading the same magazine or newspaper article or book or watching the same TV show or movie.*

   After you've finished take turns summarizing what you read or saw. (You may be surprised at your differing view of the "facts.")

   Then discuss what you liked and didn't like about it, how you agreed with it or disagreed with it. If your communication has been near zero, this level of nonemotional conversation will lead you toward the deeper levels.

2. *Here's another communications exercise: Divide a piece of paper into ten columns. As column headings write down any ten nouns or verbs. Make a copy of your sheet so your spouse has an identical page. Under each of the ten words, write five descriptive and appropriate adjectives or adverbs. Ask your spouse to do the same. Compare your two lists. How are they different? What does this say about your differences? Use this as a jumping-off place for further discussion that helps you get to know each other better.*

127

This is how Dennis and I did this exercise. The noun we chose was snow.

Tina: silent, powerful, wet, scary, frightening

Dennis: gentle, blanket, drifts, delicate, blizzard

Can you see how we have the basis for a good dialogue? I would want to find out how he sees snow as gentle. What is delicate about it? How has it been a blanket to him? And he might ask me when I found it frightening or scary.

3. *Check your environment for distractions to effective communication. Is there a TV in your bedroom? What schedule adjustments must you make to set aside a time each day for meaningful communication?*

4. *For the next week consciously "watch" yourself while talking. What gestures do you use that help your listener understand your message? What gestures might confuse or distract your listener? (You might ask your spouse for clarification on this issue.) What do you do or say that shows your listener that you are finished with a thought?*

Try Writing It Out

There is value in writing down your thoughts and feelings. Yes, it takes more effort, but you *can* edit for clarity. Though misunderstanding is still possible, you can omit the first potential for your message taking a wrong turn—even before it leaves your possession. In a Marriage Encounter weekend, participants write daily letters to their spouses as a means to learn to communicate for understanding.

Sometimes it seems as if the written word is a safer

tool than the spoken word. Verbalizing gets things set into motion so quickly, often before I have the chance to sort out what I really want to say. It has the potential to cause deep hurt in a second, especially if I am dealing with some sensitive areas. In personal sharing, written or verbal, you should come to better know not only your spouse but also yourself. When you write, it takes more time. It slows down your reaction time . . . feelings and wants begin to emerge, and often by the time you finish you go through a change process. You discover feelings you weren't even aware of before.

Letter writing did not come naturally to us, and we struggled trying to achieve what we wanted at least three times a week. We missed some weeks altogether, but we kept on coming back to it. It was the one time we felt we could truly express ourselves without being judgmental or being talked out of how we felt. Dennis and I continued to write those "love letters" daily for three years. I can't imagine letter writing being *the* communications method of choice for two people living together and growing together in a loving relationship. But it does have its value in many circumstances.

There is tremendous value in having just a few minutes a day for expressing who you are to your spouse. A space to exist with each other free from reason and need. Avoid using this time to present problems. They may pop up, but defer them to a problem-solving discussion. This is simply time to be for each other and to love each other unconditionally. It's difficult to do for even a few minutes a day.

SELF-GUIDED TOUR

1. *Take the time and effort to write your spouse a letter. Remember the first time you met. Express your feelings (use the chart on pages 122–123) about what you had wanted to happen. Start by thinking in terms of a rough draft. You're free to cross out and edit. Then copy it for "delivery." (Writing on a computer will, of course, make this process easier.)*

2. *As you replace negative habits of communication with positive habits, you might want to write "love letters" daily, weekly, monthly?*

Celebrate

It's time to celebrate your decision to improve communication by learning and acting upon the new habits presented in chapters 7 and 8. But even with good communication habits, you and your spouse might still be on the marriage-go-round. Why? You may know what the other is thinking—but that doesn't mean you agree.

10

Resolving Conflict

Many Christian couples who have invited Christ into the center of their marriage consider conflict to be out of the will of God for their relationship. Whether they're newlyweds or golden-agers, they carry the myth: Because we have put Christ first, we will experience unfailing peace and harmony. They mistakenly see love and disagreement as being opposites. But think about it. Love and hate are opposites. Putting disagreement in the same category as hate is like comparing apples and oranges.

Doug and Chris had just been reunited after a three-month separation when we met. While separated they had individually recommitted their lives to Christ. Now, they figured life together would be what they had always dreamed. No more fighting, bickering, or squabbling. No more tugs-of-war over spending too much money, no more charging up the credit cards, and no more having to keep up with the "Joneses." Because Jesus offers the "peace that passes understanding," they thought the bad habits of their marriage-go-round were over. Wrong! Within two short weeks they began to experience those same nagging circles again. The sad and frightening thing was that not only did they begin to doubt each other once more, but they began to doubt the reality of Christ in their lives. They hadn't discovered that they could disagree and still be Christians.

Yes, harmony is a realistic and desirable goal for a marriage. In Philippians 2:2 Paul tells his readers to live "united," in harmony, "having the same love, being one in spirit and purpose." That is addressed to all Christians; how much more should it apply to two people who are "one flesh."

But healthy harmony comes only after we grow through our differences. Harmony is not desirable if it comes at the price of one or both parties stagnating— being less than the person God called him or her to be.

Because you are an individual you are created different from any other individual, and differences create tension—a natural part of a creative marriage. Like feelings, tension itself is neutral, neither good nor bad. One of Webster's definitions of *tension* is "the act of stretching or straining." Another definition is "the state of being stretched or strained."

A violin wouldn't be a musical instrument if it weren't for tension placed on an otherwise limp string. But the string needs a specific amount of tension. Stretched too tight, any musician would get only a shrill sound. Stretched to the limit, the string will snap.

Think in terms of a marriage. If the "string" isn't taut, there's likely no real commitment to intimacy. There's surely no life or vitality. Your healthy differences are really reason to celebrate the spice in your life.

The tension might be in differing attitudes, ideas, or

goals. Actually we see that Christian marriages sometimes carry more tension than non-Christian unions because of the "third party" in the relationship. There's my will, your will, and God's will to consider and understand.

But watch out if the tension mounts, resulting in discord—unhealthy conflict. If each party takes sides against the other and digs in, the tensions accumulate. The oneness of "us" is totally lost, with each party caring only for him- or herself. Sometimes war breaks out. Sometimes the tension increases slowly; to use yet another image, the heat rises so slowly you don't realize you're simmering to death.

Brown-bag lunches seem to be a popular place for undercover conflict to rear its head. Dan's wife regularly made him sandwiches that were the envy of the rest of us who ate in the lunch room. Gastronomical delights. One day he exclaimed loudly, having bitten into a cleverly disguised luncheon "meat": a heart-shaped piece of cardboard. Dan sheepishly explained, "Well, I guess she's still a little upset about last night."

Dan got his wife's message, but there are better ways to resolve conflict and get your message across. Again we look to words—communication—to resolve conflict more satisfactorily and honorably than sabotage.

Where does a negative conflict start? Most often with an "I feel" that leads to an "I want" that is opposite from your equally strong "I want." Two self-interests act on each other and the emotions heat up.

In chapter 7 I promised you I'd return to the dining room scene the day I invited my California niece to come visit us. I had told Dennis, as best I then knew how, what I'd done, and I waited for his response.

Though I knew that we had two different "I wants" for this immediate situation, I stepped out, trusting in God and in Dennis's love for me. I'll let Dennis describe his reaction—the anger I could see on his face.

"As Tina stood there I struggled with my anger. *I have every right to be mad,* I thought. *She should ask me before she goes inviting people into our home. She's not being fair to me.*"

Dennis admits his standard script for this scenario had been to act on his anger. He'd justify retaliation—a few quick and terse words to make sure I knew of his displeasure and then silence. "Nonverbal disapproval was the punishment I usually used."

But, remember, this was not the usual scenario. When I changed my script, Dennis, in his confusion, held his tongue and sorted through his thoughts before acting on his anger. By that time, he says, "My immediate anger had diminished without my saying something hurtful or withdrawing into myself."

A Look at Anger

As with all emotions, anger in itself is not bad. Mark 3:5 describes Jesus reacting to the Pharisees' criticism of Him not keeping a strict Sabbath observance: Jesus "looked around at them in anger and, deeply distressed at their stubborn hearts, said to the man [with a withered hand], 'Stretch out your hand.' " He proceeded to heal the man.

If you analyze this scene, you see that the action seeming to flow from Jesus' anger was an act of love and compassion—not a destructive retaliation against His persecutors.

In Mark 11, a more familiar passage, Jesus drove moneychangers from the temple, the house of prayer that they had made into a "den of robbers" (v. 17). Though Jesus was overturning tables and benches, He was not exhibiting an out-of-control rage. The evening before His outburst, He "entered Jerusalem and went to the temple. He looked around at everything, but since it was already late, he went out to Bethany with the Twelve" (v. 11). He controlled His anger and only the next day acted upon it for good reason—to demonstrate that God's holiness was being disregarded by the very people who claimed to be honoring Him.

New and healthy habits of conflict resolution begin by learning to control one's anger. As you recognize and name an emotion for what it is, it begins to lose its power over you.

Think about anger; it's a reaction to something or someone. But what is love? It's not a reaction but an action. Dennis says, "I always felt forced into a reaction state of mind (often negative) rather than dealing with my concerns up front, working through them and being on the positive action side of things."

As you look to God, who is love, you can choose to "put on" love.

Do you remember Dennis's and my differing versions of the "chili affair" evening—a night without the kids that was totally ruined because what started as miscommunication snowballed into two people hurt and pouting—angry—for several days?

Dennis and I remember that incident well because we now see that it was the first time we put a stop to a bad situation by turning our attention to Christ and allowing Him to be the center of our relationship.

Something bigger than either one of us in our marriage! Think of it! In the pain of our selfishness, we recognized our need for His help and He nudged us out of our rut. In his well-titled book *Duel or Duet,* Louis Evans says that "Something bigger than self must grip us in the home."[1]

As we turned to God for strength we took hold of the promise of the Word: "Surely God is my help; the Lord is the one who sustains me" (Ps. 54:4).

What did God teach us then—and still? (It's a lesson that has to be continually acted upon.) When self is set aside, love takes its place.

When you are not feeling anger and can therefore think about it objectively, decide to deal with it differently. David Mace has two terrific ideas in his book *Love and Anger in Marriage.*[2]

1. Determine to give up your right to vent anger, to blame the other, or to use your anger to attack the other. Agree on perimeters beyond which your arguments must not go. Write out your rules, sign it, and post it in your bedroom or on the refrigerator. Because marriage is, for the most part, a private affair, there are no objective referees or judges to stop anger from getting out of control. You are responsible for defusing your emotion. Your rules might include:

- We will never hit each other.
- We will never go to bed mad.
- We will never bring in third parties to bolster our case (The kids think . . . Your mother says . . .)

---

[1]Louis H. Evans, *Your Marriage—Duel or Duet* (Old Tappan, N.J.: Fleming H. Revell Company, 1972), 57.
[2]David Mace, *Love and Anger in Marriage* (Grand Rapids: Zondervan, 1982).

- We won't walk out on an argument.
- We won't hit "below the belt" by calling each other names, using abusive language, or verbally belittling each other.

2. With your spouse, agree on a way each of you can ask for—and receive—help to work through your anger. Simply asking for help will force you to set the emotion aside. Your "enemy" becomes your teammate, the two of you working toward a loving solution to the problem that concerns both of you. The request is as simple as, "I'm angry. I don't want to be. Can you help me deal with my anger?"

Next time you feel anger rising, "put on" these habits:

1. Acknowledge it for what it is. In a healthy relationship you will allow anger to be expressed so that it does not build up and eventually explode like a volcano. (There's a world of difference between expressing anger and venting it.)

2. Slow down. Stand back and control your quick, automatic, negative response. Hold your tongue. Do not say words you are likely to regret. Just don't let them out. "Consider what a great forest is set on fire by a small spark. The tongue also is a fire . . ." (James 3:5–6).

Consider the fact that you may have misunderstood what you saw or heard. Keep an open mind to all—positive—possibilities. Mentally affirm God's purpose for unity in your marriage.

3. Choose to give your anger to Him. Try this exercise: It's virtually impossible to hold on to uncontrolled anger when you are repeating this phrase over

and over in your mind: "I give it up to you, Lord. I give it up to you . . ."

4. Ask yourself this question: "What can I do that will help—not hinder—our relationship?"

If you are the one whose spouse is angry, heed the words of Proverbs 15:1: "A gentle answer turns away wrath, but a harsh word stirs up anger."

SELF-GUIDED TOUR

1. *With your spouse, discuss the topic of anger when neither of you is feeling the emotion. Schedule a specific time, maybe Saturday morning over breakfast. In turn answer these questions: What do I do when I get angry? Then what do you do? Then what do I say?*

2. *Discuss—and then put into practice—the new habits listed above.*

Teaming Up

As you work to separate your anger from the problem, you can also separate yourselves from the problem. But at this stage it's important to identify the problem.

Parents magazine recently cited a study by a USC researcher that found that couples who could argue constructively described themselves as having satisfying marriages. The "constructive" style of argument included defining the problem up front and then finding solutions and ending the fight.

Part of identifying the problem is taking ownership of it. If one of us feels something is wrong, we need to work on "our" problem—not "your" problem.

Fifteen years ago at a marriage enrichment event we learned something from Margie and Ben, a couple who'd been married only six months. Considering their "inexperience," we could hardly believe their wisdom. They'd identified their bad habit: When they disagreed they placed the problem directly between them, Margie

on one side and Ben on the other. In this formation they quickly moved from expressing opinions to finding fault with each other's opinions, to attacking each other.

But they determined to stop that pattern and institute another. They took the problem out from between

them, moved closer to each other, and together looked at the problem. Margie said, "That way we were a team attacking a problem rather than each other." They drew the second diagram for us.

We took it a step further and added a third party,

We've tried this method and it works because our relationship is not reduced to a win-lose competition. "We" become bigger than any "it"—or problem—which always becomes of secondary importance to our working together as a team. As Martin Luther once said, "Between husband and wife there should be no question between Me-um and Te-um [mine and thine]."

When the telephone rang that afternoon and I was forced to confront my selfishness, I knew this disagreement had to be handled differently. How could we take this problem out from between us and deal with it? As I walked into the dining room, I could see Dennis was tense already. I knew it was my actions, or lack of them, that had created the situation. I admitted what I had done and suggested we talk about it. He was angry—his words and body language told me that. I tried for the first time to offer my help as he dealt with the anger. He decided to go out running.

When he returned we agreed to set the problem aside, enjoy the rest of Saturday afternoon, as we had pending plans, and pick up the discussion the next day after church over breakfast. This gave us both time to affirm our love for each other through an enjoyable event and time to think about the disagreement we had.

As we sat with coffee at a little outdoor cafe, I struggled once more to listen silently to his words and his emotions. I in turn tried to express mine. Then we shifted gears, in an effort to get beyond the feelings and decide what we should do. We agreed jointly that she could come and stay, but for only three days. We would help her relocate after that time, but our home life would remain a priority. We went home so much richer for our resolution.

We have since learned and practiced this method. When we realize something we are talking about has turned into a conflict, we signal that it's time to move into a problem-solving mode. Either of us will say, "We need to talk about this more." Then we determine if we are too involved in emotion at that moment to deal with the problem objectively. If so, we set another time and place to deal with the solution aspect of the situation. Of course, some situations need immediate attention, but you'd be surprised how very few have to be settled within the hour.

If either of us is tired, we select a later time for the continued discussion. And sometimes we try to change the mood by moving to another room or even going out. This doesn't mean we put the discussion off too long. We deal with one issue at a time and promptly, so that grudges don't have a chance to build up.

Even when we don't agree, we can still lovingly accept each other. Though we are two distinctly different people, our opinions carry equal value. We choose to see some validity in both points of view.

When disagreements arise, we are especially careful to rely on good communication habits—listening carefully, responding kindly, sticking to the topic at hand. In our concern for unity between us, we often physically move toward each other. It's hard for two people to feel unkindly when their arms are around each other.

We are responsible for owning our own attitudes, feelings, and wants and communicating them to each other. When disagreements arise "I" statements, rather than the accusatory, finger-pointing "you" variety, are especially important.

We have learned to believe each other, trusting that the other is being as forthright and honest as possible. If either of us doesn't know the answer to a question the other is asking, we don't fake it. As the saying goes, Honesty is the best policy.

We have heard some marvelous stories of how couples have found ways to break the tension of problem-solving sessions. A funny face, a tongue sticking out, or crossed eyes can be a good signal to your partner that you need a little time out. One couple said that when their conflict resolutions are getting so serious that they have started attacking each other personally, one will start quacking like a duck. They both start putting their arguments into quacks. They end up laughing so hard that for a moment they break loose from one emotion, anger, and move into a closer, more intimate one, laughter. Then they resume the negotiations. Don't do this without full agreement from your spouse, or they'll think you've lost it. Another couple uses water pistols to battle out the more serious moments.

SELF-GUIDED TOUR

1. *Do you have a problem-solving method you implement when disagreements get out of hand? What is it? (You might want to review the self-guided tours in chapter 5.) Does it work? Why or why not?*

2. *Consider your most recent conflict. Walk through the scenario of what solution could have been reached if you had tackled the problem as a team.*

3. *If you could improve on how you handle conflict, what is the first thing you would do?*

Negotiating Disagreements

Separating ourselves from the problem and looking at it together doesn't mean that Dennis and I agree on everything. We are still two individuals.

In his book *Love and Anger in Marriage,* David Mace lists four ways to negotiate a disagreement. When I read this I thought I had discovered gold. The new information reduced my lingering vestiges of fear of arguing with Dennis. I now see that I feared verbalizing my differences because I could foresee only one outcome to an argument: If we argued, he would abandon me emotionally.

As I read and internalized our options for negotia-

143

tion, I could see where I stood in relation to Dennis. Both of us could choose to act and negotiate—not simply react and run from confrontation.

Here are the four options:[3]

1. Capitulation. Here a disagreement stops because one person chooses to surrender or yield to the other. The resistance stops. Capitulation is healthy only when (1) you have thoroughly discussed the problem, both parties airing their views; (2) you are not in a pattern where a certain one of you always gives in to the other; (3) the yielder willingly gives up his or her position as a gift to the spouse—not with a martyr complex or with a tally card of "Now you owe me one."

Last summer we had three weeks for vacation. I wanted to do something different, but Dennis wanted to go back to our hometown, Duluth, Minnesota. His mother and our son live in Duluth, and I think we have spent at least part of each vacation there for the last fifteen years. After talking about it for some time I could see that it seemed to be more important for him to go there than it was for me to go someplace new. I agreed that it would be okay with me, and I would go willingly.

2. Compromise. In this scenario both parties agree to "go half way" and give up part of what he or she wants to accommodate the other. I like to see compromise as a blending of two individuals' qualities that shows the personality of the "one" unit in marriage.

Sometimes the first thing that seems to happen very naturally is, "Let's make a deal!" In the case of our summer vacation an acceptable compromise could have been reached. For example, I could have said that I will agree

---

[3]David Mace, Love and Anger in Marriage.

to go to Duluth for two weeks if we can spend the third week staying near the ocean. In a compromise, each of you gives up a little and you both gain a whole lot. I would get the excitement and adventure of someplace new and Dennis would get time in our hometown.

3. Coexistence. Here two people simply agree that their difference will not be resolved at this time. Two people agree to live in peace, setting aside this difference for the time being. We both know that the conflict will rise again at some point, and we agree that we'll deal with the issue then.

Situations arise when no agreement seems to be acceptable to both parties. In the case of what to do for our vacation, we could have delayed it, or agreed to put off the decision of where to go for a while. We would, in effect, agree that this disagreement would not divide us. Perhaps a solution will become obvious sometime in the future. In the meantime it would be helpful if we could agree on whether we should discuss this issue again, and if so, when and under what circumstances. You can see that this is not the best solution for a conflict, but it will do when you do not have all the information you need to make a decision, or it will buy you time while your emotions cool off.

4. Collaboration. This is the most satisfying of the four options and calls for a touch of inspiration. With the help of God, two people come up with what seems the perfect solution to the problem—a solution neither of them was likely to have thought of alone. In the atmosphere of prayer and through the process of deep sharing, a discovery is made—the cause for true celebration.

We were pleased to find a way to satisfy both of us during our last vacation. I had heard that Madeline Island in Lake Superior is a beautiful place to spend some time. It is only about a hundred miles from Duluth, and neither of us had been there before. It was within our budget, and we found out that Dennis's mother had never been there either. Dennis also suggested that we drive through Canada on our way back and see a part of that country that was new to both of us. I believe that when we are sensitive to each other, and open to different solutions, collaboration can be the rule rather than the exception.

Several, if not all, possibilities should be discussed before a decision is made. What are the pros and cons of each scenario?

SELF-GUIDED TOUR

1. *With your spouse, look at a current conflict the two of you have. Note, if either of you feels anger as you consider this topic, turn back to pages 134-138 and work to set aside your angry emotions. Don't go on if anger is controlling what you say or do. Consider this conflict in terms of the first three methods for resolution described above.*
   a. Try working out a compromise.
   b. What would happen if one of you capitulated?
   c. What would happen if you agreed to disagree?

2. *If none of these routes seems satisfactory, spend more time simply communicating with each other. Explore how each of you came to your opinions. Get to know your spouse better.*

Stop and ask the Lord to help you find a way to settle this issue. Then give each other the freedom to talk about any ideas that come to mind. Be open to considering new innovative solutions to your situation. You might be surprised at the inspiration that comes.

Ending a Disagreement

A healthy disagreement, like a story, should have a beginning, a middle, and an end. When it's over, it's over. When we are resolving a conflict, we don't let the discussion run on indefinitely. We've decided that a problem-solving discussion shouldn't last more than an hour (the shorter the better). Then take a break. Renew your love for each other; this disagreement should not interrupt that love. Set a time to get back to the issue, perhaps later that day.

When you've come to some resolution, make up and bury the argument. The only use for an old argument is to help you not make the same mistake again. Remember, a disagreement is easier to resolve than an argument. Keep it from escalating into an emotionally charged argument by using your new skills early at the disagreement stage. It's much easier to douse a brush fire than to extinguish a forest fire.

Now is the time to focus more than ever on the desired positive changes you are going to make. It's not the time to moralize or lecture on what you think happened—or should have happened.

Dennis summarizes the end of our conflict over inviting guests: "Tina and I have agreed that we want our home to be a place of God's hospitality. I asked God to forgive my selfish reactions and need for control and I extended that forgiveness to Tina in her need to please others at my expense. Today I trust Tina to tell me whom she's thinking of inviting. I try not to respond in a negative way. We are able to be open and loving with each other, especially with guests in our home." Dennis and I truly came up with a compromise in our resolution concerning my niece's coming to stay. He would have enjoyed seeing her briefly but not having her stay, and I probably would have let her stay indefinitely. So by letting her stay for a designated amount of time (three days), both of us felt we had gotten a little of what we wanted.

We returned home after that significant breakfast to a ringing telephone. It was my niece, saying she could not come at this time. One might say it had been a wasted argument, but we celebrated our success in breaking a bad habit and finding a new skill.

SELF-GUIDED TOUR

1. *Divide your last fight into its beginning, middle, and end. Did it have an end? If not, what can you do to bring it to a resolution?*

   As you work to improve your methods of conflict resolution, don't try to sit down and resolve every difference between you in one day or even one month. Yes, your new habits of communicating, dealing with anger, and resolving conflict can replace the old, but every issue that causes tension between you needn't be faced head-on immediately. Believe us, the conflicts that are most important will surface

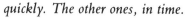

quickly. The other ones, in time.

As you work through even one area of conflict, allow yourselves the freedom to rejoice over one victory—like Jesus and the angels rejoicing over one lost sheep who returns to the fold.

11

Practicing New Skills

*I*t's one thing to have a head knowledge of new skills that could or should replace the old habits. It's another thing to act on them—to practice them until they become second nature. James 1:22–24 says:

> Do not merely listen to the word, and so deceive yourselves. Do what it says. Anyone who listens to the word but does not do what it says is like a man who looks at his face in a mirror and, after looking at himself, goes away and immediately forgets what he looks like.

Making plans to change must precede change. But then come the actual encounters when the new skills must be put to use. We've shared with you the good news—that new skills can be learned. Now comes the hard part: It takes work to put them into practice.

When Dennis and I went to a workshop where we—for the first time—listened to good communicators, we made a decision to be more open and loving in our communication. At that seminar we received, read, and even understood the map. We had an advantage over

151

some couples in that we both received the same map at the same time. Together we made the decision to follow the map that would lead us to better communication.

Even so, the decision to follow it and our ability to read the road signs and stay on the right roads would be put to the test again and again. At each crossroad we had to choose to practice the new skills we'd learned. We both remember one of our first feeble attempts.

On Friday nights we always went out for pizza—Marcella's special without the anchovies. The kids were teens and this one night of the week, they took care of themselves. This was a highlight of our week and we anticipated the good times we usually had there.

As our conversation progressed, Dennis started to talk about his new responsibilities as Sunday school superintendent. This was the weekend of the fall kick-off. For an opening "assembly" all the children, about eighty, from grades K through twelve, would gather in the sanctuary before going to their new classes.

Though Dennis wasn't used to public speaking, especially when the audience was children, he was willing to give this his best shot. After all, it's what the Sunday school superintendent always did. But what would work best? How could he entertain the young ones and still challenge the teens?

He'd spent considerable time working through his ideas and, after we'd ordered the pizza, he brought up the subject, asking my opinion of his proposed tack.

Dennis remembers the scene well: "I don't think I had spoken more than two or three sentences before she shook her head negatively and said curtly, 'Too wordy.'

"I was stunned. I hadn't even begun to share my thoughts before she had judged me and found me lacking. My shock quickly turned to unbelief. How could she make such a final judgment with so little information? The hurt was immediately followed by anger, which was evident by my facial expression and stony silence.

"We sat there in silence for the longest time as my anger intensified to the point where I wanted to hurt her back. And I knew that my silence and withdrawal was my best weapon. Glaring at Tina I saw a tear forming in the corner of her eye. She regretted her reaction. Though I was succeeding in punishing her, I wasn't happy with what I was doing."

If Dennis was stunned by my "too wordy," believe me, I was stunned by his reaction. I was only trying to be helpful. I had such great ideas to share. (I was more experienced with children than he.) I didn't mean what he thought I meant. I was simply thinking about what I'd say if I were the new Sunday school superintendent. How could something so "right" turn out so "wrong"?

What was I feeling? Surprise, fear, guilt, loneliness, confusion, and finally anger. After all, he *had* asked my opinion. I gave him what he wanted and he shouldn't be so sensitive and blame me for this.

The contradictory feelings jumbled in my mind. No. It was my fault. I hadn't listened very well. I wasn't very sensitive. I wanted our camaraderie to resume, but then there was my pride to contend with. I wanted to run. I wanted to apologize. But I just sat there and let a tear flow down my cheek toward my big mouth.

Our pizza came and got cold before either of us touched it or made a move toward the other. Both of us had time to think. We'd agreed to work to implement new habits of communication and conflict resolution and here we were, stewing in our usual silent anger.

It was Dennis who finally spoke. "That was a pretty crummy thing to say." Those words may not sound like the "perfect" words of reconciliation, but the accusatory tone of voice and deadly "you" were held back. The words and tone showed his hurt more than his anger. It was an attempt at being vulnerable, not at defending his position against me.

My attempts at communication were also feeble. After a long pause I mustered, "But you asked for my opinion."

I could tell how hard it was for Dennis to open up and explain himself, "Well, yeah . . . but I don't think you gave me a chance to say anything. You cut me off too fast."

Could I be honest and yet kind? After another long pause I said, "I didn't mean to do that. I surprised myself. I thought it was too wordy for kids."

Dennis was silent a long time, trying to work through his anger. "Okay. I want your opinion, but I need to talk out my ideas first. What I started to tell you wasn't a finished speech, just some thoughts. I've never done anything like this before and I'd rather not be doing it now. You know how nervous I am about this."

"No. I didn't realize how nervous you were. You never told me. I guess I've done this kind of thing so many times that it doesn't bother me." The pause was long. "This is really important to you, isn't it?"

Tension rose in Dennis's voice: "Sure it's important . . . I want to do a good job, but I'm worried about talking to so many kids." After another pause and in a soft voice Dennis allowed me to see a vulnerable place inside him. "I know you'd do a much better job at this than me."

As I listened to him, I was genuinely surprised at this admission because I had always seen him as being very confident in anything he attempted. But I tried hard to be a good listener. I didn't know what to say anyway, I felt so awkward. So looking at him, I reached across the table and touched his hand.

As the Proverb said, the softness of our words was turning away the anger. And I said, "I didn't intend to hurt you . . . Are you still angry?" I wanted to know Dennis's feelings.

Though it was still hard for Dennis to get it out, he was able to articulate what had happened. "I was amazed at how fast you came to your conclusion. It stung and I wanted to hurt you back. But hurting you back only complicated things and made me feel worse."

I also expressed my feelings. "I feel so alone and afraid. I wish I could erase those two little words. I really put my foot in my mouth this time."

Dennis finally could manage a little smile. "I do get a little long-winded at times. And I did ask for your opinion. My reaction surprised me. I'm sorry if I hurt you. I don't want to do that."

"What kind of pizza is this? I think my appetite is coming back!"

In the weeks and months that followed this evening, we had many opportunities to purpose to go the new way. The new ways didn't come naturally but took conscious effort.

The Awkward Stages

Think of the life progress of a talented musician. When you go to the concert hall you see and hear the results of years of practice and effort. If you are now suffering through the first year or two of a child's music lessons, you know the pain and awkwardness that every musician's parent went through at the very beginning of the "career." The song that satisfies the spirit because it is in tune and played with gusto comes after years of often awkward practice—trying to get it right.

Dennis is a saxophone player. When I met him he was playing in a band called the Evening Stars. They played for school dances and anywhere else that would have them. But he didn't learn to play well by simply thinking it was a good idea, or by reading a how-to book, or by just buying a sax. He began by making some pretty awful squeaks and squawks—as a beginner with a saxophone that was easy. Having to learn to make a good sound, read music, and develop some technique took hours, weeks, months, even years of practice. Eventually, he became very good.

Where does a novice musician start? With something easy but something very concrete. The teacher gives a certain scale to learn, a certain song to play. John Dryden said, "Mighty things from small beginnings grow."

Change is easiest when it involves small and comfortable shifts of daily habits, when you start with modest goals that are "increased" as you meet them.

Sam and Shirley sat facing each other on one of those cold stone benches in the local shopping mall. Occasionally they raised the volume of their voices. When they realized that passersby were looking at them, they self-consciously lowered their voices and continued what seemed to be an animated discussion.

This couple had deliberately chosen the shopping center as their "fight site." After repeatedly losing their tempers at each other and regretting the harsh and angry words, they fortuitously found that neither of them would carry on like that in public. Eventually when either of them felt the tension build, he or she suggested a trip to the mall. "At least that way we can't yell and scream, extending the hurt for days," said Shirley.

As their new resolution conflict skills matured to the point where the new patterns were habitual and natural, they could discontinue the trips to the mall. They could move on to their next goal, which was facing a disagreement in the privacy of their own home—without losing control of their anger.

In chapter 5, I described Marilyn and Tony whose relationship had totally broken down. No matter what Marilyn wanted to do, Tony said no and wanted to do the opposite. Anticipating his negative response she learned to bypass him, making decisions on her own without discussing them with him.

To establish some trust between them and practice communication skills, they set aside time to talk about selected nonthreatening subjects.

On slips of paper each wrote out possible topics of interest to them—nature, mountain climbing, sunsets, snow, dreams of the future, the best part of your day, the silliest thing that happened to you. Three times a week, after the kids had gone to bed, they'd pull out one or more randomly drawn slips of paper and discuss the topic. In this setting that had no threat of a win-lose situation, they talked and listened, learning more about the other.

They say it was tough. Awkward. Feeling they wanted more support, they went to a marriage workshop, where they met other couples working on their marriages.

Bill and Ellen were two people living under one roof but not sharing a life. They were like ships passing on the sea. They were within sight of each other but they never made contact. Affection had been lost twenty years ago.

As they identified some problems in their marriage, they had to negotiate a specific course of action that both were comfortable with. Though they felt they were going back to kindergarten, they first had to identify what actions either viewed as a sign of affection. Hugging? Kissing? Touching? Playing? Intercourse? The scars of their relationship were so deep. What if Bill was agreeable to give a particular sign of affection—with which Ellen was uncomfortable?

Even after they'd identified the problems of their marriage, they had to thoroughly explore the solutions and break them down into baby-step potential solutions. What might work to bring them closer to each other?

Bill and Ellen broke the deadlock by taking specific, yet awkward, steps that would make new patterns of behavior habitual. After Ellen communicated to Bill that she felt lonely even when Bill was at home, Bill, with her agreement, decided he would physically reach out and touch her every time he passed her in the house.

Bill acknowledged that he felt alone and isolated because he often ate alone. By the time he got home from the office, Ellen had already eaten with the kids. He'd eat in the company of the newspaper or TV. With his permission, Ellen agreed to wait and eat with Bill on Tuesday nights.

These changes may seem minor but they were the cause of great celebration. The first night they ate together was the first time in years they'd purposed to do anything as a couple. Hope was in sight!

Judy and Larry, in chapter 7, fought, even if they really agreed with each other. Their negative habits were firmly entrenched and at first they could make only a small step toward change. Together they agreed that the next time they started to fight and blame each other, they would change one word of their accusations. Instead of saying "you," they would say "we." "You started this fight . . ." became "We started this fight . . ." That little change transformed and defused the next fight and implanted hope in their outlook for bigger changes.

Picking Ourselves Up

Today you may not have chosen love over selfishness, "we" over "me." Today you may have fallen back into old bad habits, not "putting on" the new. Does that mean you slide back into despair, thinking the marriage-go-round is automatically spinning again—eternally, hopelessly?

No. The apostle Paul, the same man who admitted that he didn't always do what he wanted to do, wrote these words describing his life: "Forgetting what is behind and straining toward what is ahead, I press on toward the goal to win the prize for which God has called me heavenward in Christ Jesus" (Phil. 3:13–14).

Gandhi understood the importance of pressing on into the future when he said, "In undertaking a journey it is important not to lose sight of one's destination."

What is your ultimate marital destination or goal? Intimacy. Just the fact that you've gotten this far in this book indicates that you have progressed toward your goal.

Though that remains your long-term goal, you, individually and as a couple, might want to evaluate your short-term goals every month or six weeks. If a plan for instituting new habits isn't working, maybe you need another plan. If you see no results, maybe you need to make your goals smaller so that you can see the progress you're making.

Just don't despair and give up the hope that God has placed within you. Press on. Look up to the One who loved you enough to die for you just as you are. Today is the first day of the rest of your life.

SELF-GUIDED TOUR

1. *Carefully look at one or more bad habits you identified and have chosen to stop. Redefine the bad habit answering this question: How did it stop the flow of love between you and your spouse?*

2. *What concrete, short-term plan of action can you take to replace the bad habit with a good habit? If you don't _____ (bad habit), what can you do?*

   a. _____
   b. _____
   c. _____

3. *When will you begin to put this plan into action?*

12

Smoothing Out the Rough Spots of Change

*I*f you have ever been a chain smoker, you know how change in one area can affect your whole life.

Julio had been smoking since high school when he tried to stop—doctor's orders. When he set out to break the bad habit, he knew the going would be tough—but not as tough as it turned out to be. The smoking affected more aspects of his life than he had ever realized.

For instance, Julio used to stop at the 7–11 on his way home from work—to buy cigarettes. His wife, Marie, knew this and would frequently ask him to pick up things she was low on—milk or bread. Though Julio no longer buys the cigarettes, Marie still asks him to stop off at the store, where he has to steel himself against the temptation to buy a pack.

Then there's the matter of hunger. Julio now says he feels hungry all the time and he complains that Marie never has anything satisfying in the refrigerator.

And bowling on the church league. He used to enjoy

the evening out. Now the smoke in the air really bothers him.

It's just a little thing, but Julio doesn't like talking on the phone anymore. He always lit up a cigarette when he sat down for a conversation. Now he doesn't know what to do with his hands.

And fighting with Marie. When they argued, he used to pull out a cigarette for comfort. He says, "Now I can't even have a smoke when I'm upset. And that makes me feel even more depressed."

That's Julio's side of the story. Marie has a version of her own. "I was so glad when the doctor told him to quit. I believed my prayers had been answered. But now I can't believe how this has disrupted our relationship. My grocery list has changed, gotten bigger. I have to make the extra runs myself, for milk and bread, at least for the time being.

"Julio's grumpy a lot. He doesn't want to do many of the things I've taken for granted, like bowling or just going for a drive. He never calls me from the office anymore. I think he's feeling sorry for himself. And there's nothing I can do about that."

As you can see, stopping a bad habit can have many unexpected side effects. What's true for smokers—ex-smokers—is true for husbands and wives trying to break bad habits in the way they relate to each other. Stop a bad habit and both you and your spouse will have to deal with the fallout.

Actually, things could get worse before they get better.

"Our marriage is worse now than before we got some help." In fact, Sally and Jonathan were not even living together at this point. They'd started to initiate change and the unhappy situation escalated.

Jonathan and Sally had been married for about two years when things started to get rocky. To get married Jonathan had dropped out of college. He planned to return later, once they were established, but they never seemed able to stay above water financially. He had gotten a job as a shoe store manager, his salary was low. They had both grown up in well-to-do families, and their expectations of having things were difficult to live up to. A baby on the way, a new home, and a new car soaked up all their money. To cut costs they rented a small house from her parents at minimal rent. Even so, his plans for a business degree grew dimmer and dimmer.

When Sally quit her job to care for their first child, Jonathan became moody and withdrawn, the reality of their financial condition stealing his energy and attention. They had turned to the credit cards and habitually used them to get whatever they wanted. They each had one and neither of them let on to what they were really buying.

Sally had her own coping response: She spent more and more time with her parents. She'd go over in the morning and stay for the day. When Jonathan came by to pick her up, he'd be "forced" to stay for dinner. This became the routine three or more times a week, and they had no outside social activities.

When Jonathan's employer asked him to work more evening hours, he agreed. After all, they needed the money and he didn't enjoy spending all that time with her family. Then he found other evening "excuses": After work he'd hang around with his co-workers, and he signed up for an evening physical fitness program at a local health club.

Spending less and less time together, the couple's relationship grew more distant. Seeing the distress, Sally's parents paid for them to go on a marriage enrichment weekend, where they talked about where they wanted to go as a couple. For the first time in two years, they really talked. They identified several bad habits in their relationship. Certainly they discovered that part of their financial difficulty came from not talking to each other about their spending. That brought up the topic of communication. They had not been listening to each other. They realized that they seldom had a night out together and that they had no friends, no other couples their age to spend time with. They purposed for this weekend to be the beginning of change in their relationship. Yes, this was the help they had needed.

For several months they revived their enthusiasm for this new life together. But it didn't take long for the old habits to creep back, now with a sinister twist: They knew there was something better for them. The marriage-go-round hurt more than it had before. Things disintegrated until they decided they needed to separate for a short time to sort out the future of their marriage.

During the separation of several weeks they were daily in touch with us and each other. They quickly learned some significant lessons about change in their marriage.

There is truth in the opening line of Scott Peck's book *The Road Less Traveled*: "Life is difficult."[1] And

---

[1] Dr. Scott Peck, *The Road Less Traveled* (New York: Simon and Shuster, 1978), 15.

life can be most difficult when you try to change a basic habit of marriage.

Growth means giving up a relatively simple and effortless life for a more demanding one in which you reach out and assume responsibility for new actions.

Sally and Jonathan's efforts to change appeared to have failed because, though they heard and considered new ways, they did not implement them. They did not begin that first new day—and subsequent days—by acting on new habits. Instead, they lived in a dream world based on wishful thinking: "It will automatically be different now that we've decided it should be different." Because the process for change did not get established, they short-changed their attempts to start a new life together.

Stopping your marriage-go-round *and* establishing a new direction requires all four steps for change:

1. Identifying bad habits. This is probably the easiest part of the change process. On the marriage enrichment weekend Sally and Jonathan recognized several areas where they needed to change.

2. Stopping bad habits. It is probably one of the most difficult tasks you will ever attempt. This is where Sally and Jonathan fell apart. They tried for a week or so to stop but never succeeded.

3. Discovering new skills. This is probably the next easiest part. Any one of us can pick up a book or turn on the TV and discover a different way to deal with a problem. Sally and Jonathan had learned a new way to communicate on the marriage weekend. They had even talked about a new budget.

4. Practicing these new changes. Now, this is the second hardest part of this process. Sally and Jonathan

never got this far. It was too awkward and they did not make time in their schedule to practice.

Change takes time. Marriage-go-rounds don't start spinning overnight and a couple doesn't walk off down a peaceful garden path in a day. It took Sally and Jonathan nearly three years to get into their mess, and it would take them two more years to finally get on an even keel.

Don't be surprised if some change is not visible to the naked eye. During their separation it was hard to see any progress being made. But deep things were happening, especially to Jonathan. God was at work, healing past wounds and showing Jonathan the man God had created him to be. One morning he knew it was time to try again. It was nothing definite or dramatic, but he found new energy and hope.

Change can start with a shift in our attention and priorities. Jonathan shifted his focus away from his preoccupation with financial security and his disillusionment over his lost dreams of college and he looked at reality: God had given him a wife, whom he loved and who loved him, and a son. His attention turned to the kind of life that was in their grasp.

They agreed that to survive, their family unit needed to be more independent from Sally's family. They needed a couple identity. The decision to move was hard. For Sally it meant an emotional and physical break with her mother. For Jonathan it meant an added financial burden. The household budget was stretched to the limit. The first month or two they wondered if the gain was going to be worth the pain. They felt as if they were being punished; each wanted to blame the other.

They learned that feelings are not a legitimate gauge

166

to measure growth—or intimacy, for that matter. With persistence and encouragement they made it through the difficult transition until new habits were firmly established.

Today Sally and Jonathan have a healthy relationship. What a joy for us to see them grow, becoming vital members of the Christian community and models for other couples.

SELF-GUIDED TOUR

1. *When you are facing difficulties with the new way, check yourselves.*
   - [ ] *Are you handling the rough spots together?*
   - [ ] *Look at yourself. Are you resisting change? How?*
   - [ ] *Are you too bossy with your spouse? Remember, some resistance is normal.*
   - [ ] *Is there another way, another short-term goal that will get you to your long-term goal?*
   - [ ] *Have you approached the new way as an invitation to your spouse to respond rather than one more item for disagreement?*
   - [ ] *Are your goals small enough?*
   - [ ] *Try setting up an incentive to practice this new way. Treat yourselves to dinner out or to a movie for even the smallest accomplishment.*

2. *Look for guidance and encouragement in Scripture. Check out:*
   Isaiah 30:15
   Galatians 6:9
   Isaiah 41:13
   Joshua 1:9

Romans 4:20–21
James 1:12

What If My Spouse Doesn't See the Need for Change?

As I said previously, it is rare for two people simultaneously to see a bad habit and agree to sit down and make concrete plans for change. And once your eyes have been opened to the possibility of intimacy and harmony, your discontent may simply increase. Again, things are likely to get worse before they get better. But in the meantime we suggest the following plan of action, which is really a summary of the principles in this whole book:

1. Stop thinking your spouse is the whole problem.

2. Accept the fact that the Lord is starting a new work—with you. It may be true that your spouse isn't listening, but the Lord does have your attention. Seize the opportunity for your growth. "But it's so unfair," you may say. Who said life was going to be fair? God's ways are higher than ours. He knows where to start His good work. "[Be] confident of this, that he who began a good work in you will carry it on to completion until the day of Christ Jesus" (Phil. 1:6).

3. Release control of the change you want for your marriage. Hand over to God the control you have wanted so badly in your spouse. God knows your spouse better than you do and He sees the changes that are too internal and small for you to see. If God is calling you to make changes in yourself, trust God with the results of that change; He knows the effect one small change can have in your loved one's life.

4. Place your partner in God's hands. "God, our marriage isn't working for me right now. Help me to see how I can change. I put myself and _____ in your hands for you to change."

5. Be refreshed and affirmed daily in prayer. Focus on Christ and His perfect love. Your spouse may not be available to encourage you on your new path, but God is. He's the real thirst-quencher when you're needing a drink.

6. Rededicate your energies to God's answer for this relationship. Prayerfully review your commitment to your marriage. Do you want this marriage to work? Focus on doing God's will, not only on your own wants or your spouse's.

7. Forgive your partner, start each day with a clean slate. Consider what God has provided for you. Can you do any less for your life's partner?

8. Regularly reassure your spouse of your love. This doesn't mean you have to condone the negative behavior. It does mean you show your appreciation for the grace of God evident in him or her. Again, don't demand change; allow your spouse the respect of entering into the change process at his or her own speed.

There's great freedom in this plan of action. With your lover in God's hands, you don't feel compelled to know every little change God may be making in him or her. Instead, you can focus on what God is saying to you. "It is God who works in you to will and to act according to his good purpose" (Phil. 2:13). He is making you into the image of His Son.

Finding Support for Change

Walking on a new path is easiest when you have the support of family and friends who love you and care about seeing your marriage thrive. In previous chapters we've given negative examples—stories of people who turned to parents or friends to gain support against a spouse or to find refuge. These are unhealthy patterns, but the healthy alternatives are not familial isolation: You and me against the world.

The encouraging word or suggestion from a trusted observer can spur you on when change seems particularly hard, though it's important to take any outside suggestions straight to the One who is in charge of your change. The loving Lord knows your situation best. Friends or family can be unsettled or frightened by your pain or attempts at change. Sometimes they'll say anything if they think it will make the pain go away. And we've learned that everyone has an opinion on how a marriage should work. The more opinions you get, the more confusing a picture can become.

The kind of friends you need on your side are those who won't let you off the hook, who won't let you take the easy way out, who continuously challenge you to improve your relationship. Often your pastor can be that kind of guide. Dennis and I hope we have been friends of this kind to a couple we grew up in the faith with. Through a very difficult period in their family life, we were there to encourage them. It was not an easy path they chose, and we had to come to grips with our faith too. But we continue to support their decision and point them to their goal of a deeper commitment in marriage.

We've made valuable friendships in marriage enrichment groups, couples that agree to meet together for the express purpose of helping one another strengthen their marriages. Here you will find support to plan and see yourselves through the change process.

You can find such a group by checking your telephone book under Marriage Encounter, or A.C.M.E. (Association of Couples for Marriage Enrichment). Check with your pastor. Perhaps your church has such a group, or maybe you could start one. Pastors love to hear from couples who want to improve their relationships.

SELF-GUIDED TOUR

1. *To whom can you turn for encouragement and support as you implement the changes in your marriage?*

2. *As you look to God, desiring to do His will, hold on to Romans 8:28: "We know that in all things God works for the good of those who love him, who have been called according to his purpose."*

13

Celebrate Your Marriage

*B*ecause of the Lord's great love we are not consumed, for his compassions never fail. They are new every morning; great is your faithfulness. (Lamentations 3:22–23)

Our dog Tinker ran ahead of us, frantically chasing dried leaves, the last remnants of autumn withered and marooned on the snow-covered lake. Sunlight cut through the crisp air as Dennis, I, and the children eagerly stepped out onto the ice. The trek was an adventure promising to yield hidden secrets, mysteries not experienced in summer's heat.

Halfway across, I paused and listened to the silence of snow. Tinker was only a small black speck against the horizon. The children were way out ahead, flailing their arms, making angels in the snow. Ahead of us white hills and beaches stretched as far as I could see.

Dennis and I kept walking, hearing only the crunch of our snow boots. Walking in the snow was hard work, but we kept going, fixing our eyes on that distant shore.

As if rehearsed, we both made an abrupt about-face,

protecting our faces from a frigid gust of arctic air. We stood still, our backs to the wind until the icy blast subsided. In that instant our mittened hands reached out for assurance. Holding hands, our eyes met, then looked up to glance over the way we had come. Stretching out to the shoreline was the beautiful and humorous imprint of our family. At first the prints were orderly and purposeful; we'd played follow the leader. They were playfully chaotic when a snow fight had erupted. Right at our feet were the wing-spread snow angels.

That moment is locked in time for me. I had a fleeting insight into what marriage, family, and God are all about, and I joyfully celebrated what I saw.

But it was just a moment. With a giggle and a snowball sailing past us, that window of timelessness slammed shut. Dennis and I turned back into the wind, scooped up a handful of snow, and ran into our future.

Months later, in a totally unrelated conversation, Dennis and I referred to that day—that glance. As we shared, the moment came alive again. The creativity of that moment went beyond that time and place. Though neither of us then had known what the other was thinking, we had both been touched with a grace that drew us closer together. We could see the elements of marriage come together: love and creativity, shared destiny, mystery, and intimacy.

Such epiphanies don't happen often, yet they symbolize the truth that marriage is meant to be a celebration of life and creative love, our love for each other and God's love for us: He loved us before we loved Him. It is a love that frees us and empowers us to give of ourselves and thereby empower others.

The Creative Power of Love and Shared Destiny

In talking about her husband, Charles, Anne Morrow Lindbergh noted this power of love:

> To be deeply in love is, of course, a great liberating force and the most common experience that frees. . . . Ideally, both members of a couple in love free each other to new and different worlds. I was no exception to the general rule. The sheer fact of finding myself loved was unbelievable and changed my world, my feelings about life and myself. I was given confidence and strength. The man I was to marry believed in me and what I could do, and consequently I found I could do more than I realized.[1]

There is creative power in unity and shared purpose. When you know someone is cheering for you, you do have more confidence and strength. I know this because when I returned to college after twenty years of mothering and homemaking, I was frightened. I lacked intellectual confidence. Dennis was my own personal cheerleader. For five years he strengthened me with his belief in my abilities. He pushed me when I was at a standstill, thinking I would never finish. He helped me when I fell down or messed up an assignment. He held me when I was afraid. With him by my side I went further than I had ever imagined I could. I finished my B.S. and went on to get not just one graduate degree but two!

---

[1]Charles Swindoll, *Growing Strong in the Seasons of Life* (Portland, Ore.: Multnomah Press, 1983), 66.

SELF-GUIDED TOUR

Celebrate your marriage by identifying a time when you felt strengthened by the love and support of your spouse. Share this incident with your spouse.

The Creative Power of Mystery

There is also creative power in the mystery of marriage. No matter how well you learn new communication skills, you'll never know and understand all there is to know about this unique person you married.

Lowell O. Erdahl, a pastor and bishop of the Evangelical Lutheran Church in America, and his wife, Carolyn, describe the mystery in marriage that leads us into new vistas: "A sense of mystery and a bit of awe in each other's presence makes life a more exciting adventure. In our marriage such reverence for the mystery of life keeps us from settling down in the dull satisfaction of having arrived . . . we are always on the way."[2]

The very foundation of marriage is a mystery: Two shall become one—a mystery. Male and female, He created them—a mystery. In His image, He created them—a mystery.

Dennis and I have learned so much about good communication skills. I know him so well, but even with that knowledge of him, I choose to hold on to the reverence of the mystery—the unique and growing person—that he is.

I value the mystery of his memory—so different

---

[2]Lowell and Carolyn Erdahl, *Be Good to Each Other; An Open Letter on Marriage* (New York: Hawthorn Books, Inc. , 1976), 74.

from mine. We remember different kinds of things. I'll remember as if it happened yesterday certain details of events that happened years ago. I know, for instance, that the spread on our honeymoon bed at the cabin on Crystal Lake in Wascott, Wisconsin, was a pinkish beige, knobby chenille.

Dennis doesn't remember those personal details but he's a master at Trivial Pursuit, having things he's read or heard on the tip of this tongue.

Dennis says he's amazed by my ability to envision what something will look like—if we just do x, y, and z. How easy it is for me to redecorate a room—if Dennis does the manual work. I don't understand how Dennis computes all the logistics of the final project, but I don't need to, as his work serves as the finishing complement to my original designs for the project.

Does seeing the value of Dennis's uniqueness diminish my own value? No. God has created Dennis and me as pieces of the beautiful and intricate universe. Celebrating my marriage includes celebrating the mystery of God's creative talents in making Dennis. With God's help I have freed him to be who he is—not who I need him to be.

SELF-GUIDED TOUR

Celebrate your marriage by identifying one mystery about your spouse that you appreciate. Share this with your spouse.

The Creative Power of Intimacy

Again, David Mace has described intimacy as "shared privacy." This shared privacy is a major element in sexual activity. Though one might be ashamed to parade nakedly in front of strangers, family, or friends, such inhibitions melt in the intimate privacy protected by marital bonds.

But it goes beyond the physical aspects of a relationship and to the very heart of our emotional and spiritual beings, which can be intertwined.

Just as a couple does not live in a constant state of sexual arousal, even the best marriage has moments of intense emotional intimacy, which then wane. In *Close Companions* David Mace describes the pattern of intimacy and distance, which are a part of the mystery created when two people—ever changing in temperament and insecurities—live together.[3]

The intimacy elements of two becoming one often call for one or both parties to make concerted effort and set aside "quality" time. The communication skills previously discussed must be honed and trust built up.

But then occasionally the intimate moment takes you by surprise and may even descend in silence, as it did for Dennis and me on the icy lake.

To help you recognize the grace of intimacy in your own marriage, we've asked other couples to describe celebratory moments of intimacy that encourage them when they need a reminder of the hope that is theirs. Here are some of the great responses:

- Watching my wife as she prepared breakfast for me and the kids, being struck by her commitment to our life.
- My husband calling to say he had taken the after-

---

[3]David Mace, *Close Companions* (New York: The Continuum Publishing Company, 1982), 92.

noon off so we could have some uninterrupted time together just to "be."

- My husband walking in the door after facing a huge problem at work. That morning I'd knelt in my garden and prayed for him. The moment our eyes met, I knew the prayer had been answered.
- The first time we could not agree on an issue, coming to a moment when we knew that Christ was our only hope. We would love each other in Him.
- Discussing our future, struggling through our diverse hopes and dreams for our life together.
- After forty-six years of marriage, sitting side by side silently watching the ocean at sunset.
- Putting the kids to bed early, building a fire, spreading a soft blanket in front of the fireplace, listening to the "Moonlight Sonata" a dozen times, and letting nature take its course.
- Going out to breakfast on Saturday mornings without the kids.
- During the birth of our third child—our eyes meeting as our son appeared. We weren't alone but we were!
- Stopping on our way home from a fund-raiser banquet—to talk and watch planes take off at the airport. One thing led to another, the windows got steamed, and a policeman knocked on the window to tell us to move along.
- Reading aloud to each other.
- Reading a loving note in my lunch box.
- Seeing a smile from across the room.
- Hearing a certain inflection in her voice.
- Feeling his touch as he walks by me in the kitchen.

You'll note that some of these special moments were unplanned and once-in-a-lifetime events. Others are more ordinary, the events that tend to get lost because there are no emotional fireworks to set them apart.

SELF-GUIDED TOUR

1. *Celebrate your marriage by identifying a once-in-a-lifetime intimate moment you had with your spouse. Share this with your spouse: I felt very close to you when . . .*

2. *Identify a more ordinary, repetitive "something" about your spouse that is cause for celebration. Share this also.*

The Adventure of Marriage

The new creative power evident in your marriage allows you to grow beyond the marriage-go-round. The upward road ahead of you is an adventure that can be new every morning.

That's because every morning you have a choice to remarry your spouse, to choose him or her again as your sweetheart.

In an early chapter we told the story of Jan who was disillusioned that Bill no longer bought her flowers and jewelry. What does she say now? "I see him differently. He does bring me gifts, but they are things like putting the clean laundry away or gently supporting me when I am nervous about my job." Jan had reason to celebrate her marriage because she chose to love Bill—every day and for the person he was.

And whom does she have to thank for this change in her? The Lord Jesus Christ to whom she turns for strength.

Most mornings you can find Dennis and me praying. We spend individual time early in the morning talking to God. Later, just before I drop him off at work, we bow our heads, hold hands and pray aloud when we get to the parking lot at Dennis's job. We block out the noises around us and practice the presence of Jesus.

A prayer may go something like this:

This is your day, Lord.

Thank you for allowing us to be a part of it.

We are grateful.

We give it back to you.

You guide us, you teach us,

You bring us together at the end of the day.

Bless Dennis (Tina), go before him (her) with your protection, your blessing, and your guidance.

And place before us your ways, for we desire to be your servants.

Amen.

Oswald Chambers says: "No matter what changes God has wrought in you, never rely upon them, build only on the Lord Jesus Christ, and on the Spirit He gives."[4]

SELF-GUIDED TOUR

Alone or with your spouse, purpose to get married every morning, renewing your faithfulness and love to God and your spouse. Celebrate your life together!

---

[4]Oswald Chambers, *My Utmost for His Highest* (New York: Dodd Mead & Co., 1935).

Afterword

*T*he self-guided tours in national parks lead you around the sites and then bring you back to where you started.

We often take the tour a second time, and when we do so we're amazed and delighted at the sights we missed. The first time through we learned the mechanics of the walk: where to go, what lookouts were available, how long the walk would take, what kind of information was offered. The second time around we could look for little surprises and enjoy the walk just for the walk.

You've now come to the end of this book and its self-guided tour. Before you put it on the shelf or in the cardboard box destined for the church rummage sale (which actually isn't such a bad place for it, as someone else will have a chance to read it), stop and take the walk one more time.

Go back and look again at the self-guided tours. What surprises are there in your answers? If you didn't write answers the first time around, how would you answer the questions now? What good times do you see to celebrate? In retrospect, what can you learn from the bad habits you identified in the first chapters of the book? (Those bad habits needn't be stacked in one big pile and labeled trash. The past contains your training for the future.)

For us, writing this book has been like penning a long letter to a friend. We have imagined who you would be and hope you have found help in these pages.

Not every wonder of God's great creation is found in every national park. We know we have left many of your questions unanswered, but we want to encourage you to continue your search for all the wonders God has planned for you.

The Next to the Last Word

Even if you choose not to take our advice to review your self-guided tours, please do yourself this one favor: Read the following appendix all the way to the end, even if you think it doesn't apply to you. Think of it this way: It might prove to be helpful to a friend. Someday the Holy Spirit might bring to your mind something you read in these few pages. Give Him this chance to work.

Appendix

Do We Need More Help?

As counselors Dennis and I are frequently asked two questions:

(1) How do we know if we need more help?
(2) Where do we go for help?

But before answering those two questions we ask couples a more basic question: If you were to seek outside help, what would you be expecting from the counselor?

Many couples get counseling for the wrong reasons and with expectations that are as unrealistic as those of a bride and groom wearing rose-colored glasses.

First, they expect to find out how to change their spouse.

Second, they expect to be "magically" released from their unhappiness. They are still looking for a Cinderella-Prince Charming escape route to life "happily ever after." As the saying goes, they want "gain" but they want to bypass the "pain." They're sure that the "right" expert with the "right" therapeutic plan will solve all their problems.

Third, they expect this helper to be a perfect model of success in every area of life. He or she must be all-part saint and no-part sinner.

Couples going into counseling with these unrealistic expectations are ultimately bucking their own progress. Their disappointments—with their own lack of progress or with the less-than-perfect performance of the "expert"—will slow down their growth toward a mature relationship.

A counselor will not work magic for you. He or she will provide guidance, evaluation, and encouragement for you individually or as a couple. If you are considering counseling, ask yourself this question: Am I willing to work to make my marriage better? (Even if your answer is no, keep reading!)

Some couples who have been spinning on the marriage-go-round will read this book and clearly see how to put on the brakes, step off, and start walking side by side on an upward path. Others will need more help to stop old, bad habits and act on new skills.

A couple does not need to be on the way to the divorce court before looking for help. If you have a chronic problem that is not under control and for which you don't see the solution, you need help.

If this is your case, consider your three options:

1. You do nothing; both spouses refuse to seek counseling—and the problem gets worse.

2. One of you gets counseling. In this scenario the "reluctant" spouse usually feels that the marriage doesn't need help. Or he or she might say, "I'm not the one with the problem. My spouse is."

If your spouse wants you to join him or her in seeking help, perhaps you could give him or her the "gift" of going—whether or not you believe you need it. Ask yourself this question: "If my spouse thinks our marriage is in trouble, what is wrong? What can I learn about my spouse or myself that will improve our relationship?"

3. Both of you go for help; this is the ideal solution.

If you have a chronic problem but see a possible solution, you might try to resolve it on your own. If you take this course, you should set a definite, timed trial period for seeking solutions. If your plan doesn't work, seek outside help.

(Review the section "A Word of Warning" and the self-guided tour on pages 79–80, chapter 5. Again, these warning signs call for action.)

Before you go for help, do your best to define the problem for which you're seeking solutions. At first glance "we fight all the time" might seem to be true, but on closer examination you might see that the issues are more specific: "We frequently fight because we cannot resolve the differences in the way we want to spend money." Or, "We cannot seem to control our anger when we have a difference of opinion."

With specific issues you want to resolve, you have a way to measure progress; you have something around which to form a plan of action. In counseling you will receive help for working through a process of reconciliation. What you learn about negotiating growth you can then learn later in any other situation.

Calling a counselor doesn't necessarily mean you're "signing on" for the rest of your married life. A number of couples call us and request one counseling session to work out a problem. They feel they need an objective third party to help them sort out issues and emotions.

Sometimes we are able to recommend a specific course of action or a marriage enrichment event, especially if their problem is a general one, such as poor communication patterns.

But more than likely a counselor will ask that you continue sessions long enough to work through a problem. (That doesn't mean therapy should drag on forever; resolution of the problem is the goal and you should progress toward that goal.)

Typically after a first session you will feel relief—over the simple fact that you have finally done something to alleviate a problem.

Don't let that initial good feeling fool you. The real work lies ahead. Changing habits will still be difficult, though you now have a guide—someone who is willing to walk with you through the change.

If you seek counseling as a couple, the counselor may ask you to go to a few separate sessions in which he or she can get to know you as individuals. The best guidance for a relationship can come after such individual assessment.

The results of change won't show immediately. Pace yourselves; be patient. Talk openly with the counselor and do any homework you're given. You're paying this person to get help that will affect your living situation back home. Don't waste your time with a counselor just being on your best behavior. You're there to get help for your worst behavior.

A counselor is a skilled listener who is able to help you see yourself as you really are. As you face up to yourself and your inadequacies, the counseling sessions may be hard, even confusing. But we encourage you to persevere—as will your counselor. Choose to grab hold of the hope that is before you. The counselor is there to help you chew "bite-sized pieces." Eventually you'll be able to do it on your own.

If you've been in—and cooperated with—counseling for six months or so and you sense nothing is happening, you might want to find another avenue of help. Not all counselors or family therapists who are easy to talk to are good at effecting change. Some won't address your particular problem as well as others.

Be fair and give the counselor the opportunity to do his or her best to help your situation, but remember that you are paying; in that sense you are in charge of your counseling.

We advise that you try to find a Christian counselor. If you cannot find a Christian counselor, at least ask your counselor how he or she feels about Christ being the agent of change in marriage. Though you can receive help outside the Christian belief system, it is important that both you and the counselor establish up front your basic value and belief systems. If they are incompatible, continue your search.

Before selecting a counselor, check the person's qualifications for giving guidance. You might get recommendations from ex-clients, the counselor's peers, or your pastor. Have a clear understanding of the cost and payment schedule of the sessions, as well as when, where, and how often they will take place.

SELF-GUIDED TOUR

1. *If you have a chronic problem that is not under control and for which you don't see the solution, what are you going to do about it this week? Can*

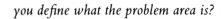

you define what the problem area is?

2. *What steps will you take to find a counselor? Whom will you call to get recommendations?*

For information about the authors' marriage enrichment retreats, please write to them in care of:

Bethany House Publishers
6820 Auto Club Road
Minneapolis, MN 55438